SQUEAKY WHEELS

SQUEAKY WHEELS

Travels with my Daughter by Train, Plane, Metro, Tuk-tuk and Wheelchair

Suzanne Kamata

ALSO BY SUZANNE KAMATA

The Mermaids of Lake Michigan

Screaming Divas

Gadget Girl: The Art of Being Invisible

The Beautiful One Has Come: Stories

Call Me Okaasan: Adventures in Multicultural Mothering

Losing Kei

Love You to Pieces: Creative Writers on Raising a Child with Special Needs

The Broken Bridge: Fiction from Expatriates in Literary Japan

SQUEAKY WHEELS

Travels with my Daughter by Train, Plane, Metro, Tuk-tuk and Wheelchair

Suzanne Kamata

ISBN: 978-1-948018-44-9

Library of Congress Control Number: 2019933342

Dedication

To my mother, who taught me
to love books and always
believed in me.

Prologue: Underground

MY DAUGHTER AND I are stuck underground. Above, the Parisian avenues are busy with honking cars and beggars and tour buses and dogwalkers. If I close my eyes, I can see them: the tourists on Segways, the taxis, the café waiters, the flower vendors. Here below, thirteen-year-old Lilia sits in her wheelchair, hands folded in her lap, while I frantically search the metro map. How do we get out of this tunnel? How will we get back up to street level and sunlight? The guy at the station said to get off *here*. He said it was *accessible*. But at this stop, a seemingly minor one since the platform has already cleared and we are all alone, there is no elevator, no gently sloping ramp. There are only steps, and my daughter can't stand, let alone walk. She is too heavy for me to carry.

I can feel patches of sweat forming at my armpits and lower back. I'm starting to feel lightheaded. Maybe we got off at the wrong stop. Maybe I misunderstood. He was speaking in French after all, and my language skills have gotten rusty. Could it be that he was warning us specifically *not* to go this way? Maybe we could get on the next train, but what if all of the stations are the same? If only I could call my husband and get him to come rescue us! But I can't, because he is back home in Japan with our son, Lilia's twin brother.

My daughter watches me. She giggles at my consternation. Extreme expressions often strike her as funny. "What? What?" she asks in English, the one word that she knows, wagging her index finger in Japanese Sign Language.

"*Chotto matte.*" I put my hand under my chin like Rodin's *The Thinker*, making the sign for "wait."

I don't want her to know that I am lost, that I am flailing, failing at my mission. She wanted to come to Paris, so I promised her years ago that I would make it happen. She wants to go to Versailles. I made a pledge to take her. And now here we are, in the metro. Stuck, like sinners in purgatory. Why did I ever think that this was a good idea? And how will we ever get out of here?

Lilia's World

MY TWELVE-YEAR-OLD DAUGHTER Lilia wants to go to France. She plucks at her shirt and signs that she wants to go clothes shopping in Paris. Fashion capital of the world! She gazes at me with her brown eyes, puts her hands together as if to pray, and says, "Iaaiii!" *Ikkitai! I want to go!*

In truth, I would love to take her. When I was about her age, I'd started studying French and dreamed of visiting Paris as well. I finally made it to the City of Lights my junior year in college. I'd been back a few times since my semester abroad, but not since I met my husband, who was convinced that the French were snooty. For a long time, I'd fantasized that when she turned twelve, Lilia and I would take a trip to Paris together, leaving her dad and twin brother behind in Tokushima.

Alas, France is very far from Tokushima Prefecture where we now live, and we are perpetually broke. Until the birth of our children, my husband Yoshi and I lived comfortably working as teachers in public schools. But when our twins were born fourteen weeks early and it became clear that our daughter was deaf and had cerebral palsy, I was forced to quit my job. At the moment, Paris is out of reach. Still, I'm intrigued by her sudden interest. I admit I may have planted a seed in her curly-haired head at some point, but for the most part, she came into this wanderlust on her own.

"How did you learn about shopping in Paris?" I ask her.

"I saw it on TV," she signs.

I was impressed that she'd picked it up on her own. She learned quite a bit from television and manga, which many parents consider junk.

A few days later, she digs into her school satchel and pulls out a flyer advertising an upcoming show at the nearby planetarium. The theme is Vincent van Gogh's *The Starry Night*, and there's a picture of the artist himself.

"*Iaaiiii!*" she says, stabbing her finger at the advertisement.

I don't tell her right then that I once visited the Van Gogh Museum in Amsterdam. I had spent some time in the city en route to a writer's conference before she was born. I went on a cruise through the canals, climbed the stairs to Anne Frank's hiding place, and took in the collection at the Rijksmuseum. I know that if I tell Lilia this, she'll add the city to her increasingly long list of places to visit, and her dad and I still haven't fulfilled our promise of taking her to Tokyo Disneyland. But I do tell her that Van Gogh was interested in Japanese art, and that he painted his own imitations of some of Hokusai's famous paintings.

She pats her chest impatiently. *"I know, I know."* And then she proceeds to sign the troubled artist's life story.

"Where'd you learn all that?" I ask her.

She puts her hands together and then opens them. *"From a book."* No doubt she read about him in one of those manga biographies that she loves. Impressed, I indicate a print of *Roses et Anemones* hanging on our wall. "That's by Van Gogh." She immediately pulls herself up onto the back of the sofa to get a better look, and nods in appreciation.

Her curiosity about the world doesn't stop there. A couple of weeks later, when my first novel is published in Russian translation, she asks me to help her find the country on the globe. And then Yoshi and I take her and her brother Jio to see the Bolshoi Circus, where she is enchanted by the cat tamer and the tightrope walkers and the spangled lady on a unicycle. She adds Russia to her list. And Hawaii, having spent hours looking at photos of Yoshi's and my wedding. We were married under a blue sky at the Pua Melia Plantation on Oahu, surrounded by purple plumerias.

She wants to go to Italy, too, after watching a travelogue on TV.

"Do they speak French in Italy?" she asks me via sign language.

"No," I reply. "Italian. 'Ciao' means 'hello.'"

She shrieks in delight and signs "Easy!" by stabbing the palm of one hand with her index finger then touching her chin. *Ciao* is the name of one of her favorite monthly manga magazines. She knows that word. And she loves pasta!

A girl after her mother's heart, I'm thinking. When I was growing up in small town Michigan, I had my own travel fantasies. I'd go to New York, first of all, and then to Australia, Egypt, Paris. I eventually went to some of those places, and also to a small farming town in Japan where I wound up falling in love.

I'm thinking that being interested in the world as she is, Lilia will love social studies. It'll probably be her favorite subject next year when she starts junior high at the School for the Deaf. She'll get to learn about all these countries—where they are, what kind of clothes people wear, what they eat.

We've had a preview of Japanese social studies classes through her twin brother, Jio. Although kids in Japanese public school don't usually start studying about foreign countries until junior high school, Jio goes to a private school with an English immersion program and an accelerated curriculum. I earn just enough money as an adjunct at a couple of local universities to cover his tuition. Although he could have gone to public school for free, the local primary school is notorious for its unruly students. Yoshi was worried that gentle Jio, with his foreign mother and disabled sister, would be a magnet for bullies. Here in Japan, incidents of bullying-related suicides and murders occasionally flare up on the news. Teachers typically ignore problems, leaving kids to "work things out by themselves."

Although I'd thought that Jio would be able to make friends in public school, I'd wanted him to continue using English and to be among international children. We were one of very few mixed-race families in our town and I wanted Jio to know that he wasn't alone. Luckily, there was one other boy of mixed parentage in his homeroom, as well as a few kids in other grades who'd lived abroad or had a foreign parent.

AT THE BEGINNING of summer vacation, Yoshi and I are asked to attend a special orientation meeting about Lilia's junior high school curriculum. She has been attending the Tokushima School for the Deaf since she was a baby. The school has an early intervention program which segues into a three-year kindergarten and continues through high school. We are lucky to live a mere ten kilometers from the only school for the deaf in the prefecture. Others have to travel from far away. Although in kindergarten there were about ten kids in Lilia's class, the numbers have dwindled as parents have chosen to mainstream their children at schools closer to their homes. One boy, who had been in the NICU at the same time as Lilia and Jio, and who was born with multiple disabilities, has died. Now there are only three kids in the sixth grade. Lilia and one other boy are multiply disabled. She has cerebral palsy and uses a wheelchair because she can't walk. The boy is autistic. The two of them are on the special education track at the deaf school.

I don't really know what this means until my husband and I, and the boy's mother, show up for a meeting in a conference room on the third floor. It's the end of July. Thankfully, the room is cooled by a wall unit. The deaf school, like most other public schools in Japan, does not have central heating or air conditioning. When it's hot, the windows are opened. Butterflies and mosquitoes—and sometimes errant birds—fly into the classrooms. The library books warp under the heat and humidity, which brings sorrow to a book lover like me. But maybe things will be different when the new school for the blind and deaf is built in three or four years.

This building is old, and bears cracks from the Great Hanshin Earthquake which struck Kobe in 1995, shaking buildings all the way over here on the island of Shikoku. Although there are four floors, and deafness is often paired with other disabilities, there is no elevator. My husband and I have complained about this time and time again, but the officials say that there is no money to build an elevator in a school that will soon be torn down. "Why don't you send your daughter to the School for the Handicapped?" they ask. If my daughter is going to go to any other school, I would want her to go to a regular public school, not a school for the physically challenged. But we insist that what is most important for our daughter—a bright, gregarious, sometimes lonely child—is communication. My husband, who no longer works at the high school where he was a baseball coach, currently teaches at the School for the Handicapped (recently re-named the Special Support School in a bid for political correctness) knows that the teachers there are not fluent in sign language. Neither are the mostly hearing students. So while she might be able to go from floor to floor in her wheelchair all by herself, she would be cut off from her first language.

We insist that she be allowed to remain at the School for the Deaf with her signing peers, kids she's known basically all of her life.

Okay, fine, the school administrators finally relent.

"She'll have to get up three flights of stairs all by herself, because the junior high is on the third floor," the head teacher tells us.

"Why can't you move the junior high school downstairs?" we ask. I mention a high school in Kobe where an entire class was moved to the first floor to accommodate one student who used a wheelchair.

There aren't enough classrooms, we are told.

It's a sprawling, cavernous school with only about forty students total. Because the students vary in ability, many study one-on-one with their teachers. But why can't the classrooms be partitioned? Or why can't the junior high school be moved downstairs and the younger kids, who can walk, moved upstairs?

The head of the junior high, who is also Lilia's at-school physical therapist, suggests that it's not as bad as we think. With effort, Lilia can make it up the stairs while hanging on to the railing. It'll be part of her daily physical therapy. She'll just have to get to school extra early. While I still have some doubts, I know that the teachers at this school, some of whom have known Lilia since she was a baby, care about my daughter. I trust that they will make things as easy for Lilia as possible.

So then there's the PowerPoint presentation about the classes that Lilia will be taking. She'll be studying Japanese, of course. And mathematics. And there will be some life-training-type courses: how to do laundry, how to prepare simple meals. These three years will go by in a flash, the teacher reminds us. We have to start getting her prepared to enter society. Find out what she's good at, think about her future.

She likes art, I think. And she's pretty good at it. Last summer, she won a prize for her painting of the Atomic Dome in Hiroshima. It was exhibited all over the prefecture, and later an image of it was published in an American children's magazine. She spends hours drawing original comics. She tells anyone who asks that she wants to be a manga artist in the future. But I know that it's difficult to make a living as an artist.

Although lately Lilia has been telling me that she wants to go to college, and I nod and say "you'll need to study really hard," no one else imagines that she will ever be able to pass the very difficult entrance examinations required by Japanese universities. It's doubtful that she will even be able to pass the rigorous exam required for entrance into a Japanese high school. I've heard Japanese parents and educators say that one can determine a child's future by the fifth grade. Although I don't believe it myself, my husband agrees that fifth grade is key: that's the year that the wheat gets separated from the chaff.

In the sixth grade, Lilia reads at about a third grade level. She can write simple sentences, but she makes many grammatical mistakes. In math, she hasn't gotten beyond multiplication. Long division still gives her trouble, while her twin brother is dipping into algebra. There is no need for Lilia to worry about the "*juken benkyo*"—studying for exams—that obsesses parents all across Japan, including the parents of Jio's classmates. Thus, there is no mention of the English, science, and social studies classes that are a part of a standard junior high school education in Japan. These are test subjects.

"There's no English," I whisper to my husband.

All this time, I've been telling my daughter that she'll have English classes from seventh grade. I've even started teaching her with a workbook so she'll have a head start. She learned how to write her and her brother's names years ago, all by herself. She can write "mama" and "love" and she knows what they mean. She knows how to say "thank you" in ASL. She says "yummy" after she digs into my spaghetti parmigiano.

"We'd like our daughter to study English," my husband says in his booming voice. As a Japanese man, he has more authority than I have, a foreign woman with a weird accent. I let him do the talking. "And social studies. Even just a little."

The head teacher and the other mother listen patiently while my husband enumerates the reasons that we'd like those subjects to be added to our daughter's study load. I would've thought they'd be obvious. Everyone knows that Lilia has relatives in the United States, that her mother is an English-speaker (although I communicate with her only in Japanese because I am the one who helps her with her homework), and that she travels with her family. I mention how, on our last visit to South Carolina, where my family lives, Lilia struggled to communicate with those around her.

She was trying to talk to my dad, her American grandfather. When she realized that he didn't understand any of her signs, she grabbed some paper and a pen and wrote her question in Japanese. My dad shrugged, uncomprehending. Finally, her cousin dashed off to find Lilia's brother Jio. He translated, and communication was achieved. Phew!

During that visit, Lilia looked up English expressions on her electronic dictionary, demonstrating her eagerness to use the language. *To communicate.* "She wants to learn," I tell the head teacher. Having attempted to teach disinterested Japanese students how to speak English for over fifteen years, I understand the importance of motivation.

"Well, thanks for bringing this up," the teacher says. "If you hadn't said anything, we wouldn't have known how you felt."

By the end of the meeting, we have hogged most of the time with our concerns about our daughter. My husband and I apologize to the mother of the autistic boy, who hasn't expressed any worries of her own. Has she accepted her son's limitations? Does she think we are being unrealistic? Generally speaking, I find Japanese people to be fatalistic. One of the most often-repeated phrases that I hear is "*Shikata ga nai*," which means "It can't be helped." To me, it's an excuse to do nothing, to fail. But there is also a do-or-die spirit here. Think of kamikaze pilots.

Although we have made our wishes known, my husband, a veteran of the Japanese education system, is pessimistic. He doesn't believe that the curriculum will be changed. It's too much trouble. The teachers are always too busy.

A WEEK LATER, I set out on a field trip with deaf school teachers and a parent or two to tour *Lemon no Ie*—Lemon House—a facility for adults with disabilities. I have mixed feelings about this outing. On the one hand, I'm interested in the lives and times of those with disabilities in Japan. On the other, I'm afraid that it will depress me. My daughter's ambitions, at age twelve, go beyond sorting screws and group-home dwelling. Every day, she shares with me her dreams of marriage and children and drawing manga and studying English and, of course, traveling to France. Her father expects that, as an adult, she will live in the bungalow originally added onto our house for my mother-in-law. "You have to tell Lilia that she won't be able to get married," Yoshi says. "She needs to face reality."

Meanwhile, I'm always trying to figure out how she can get off this small island and achieve her goals. I know that there are many people with cerebral palsy who have jobs, live independently, fall in love, marry and raise children. Japan needs to change, not my daughter.

Lemon House is only about seven miles from downtown Tokushima, the prefectural capital, but it feels very rural. The bright yellow building is set amid farmer's fields of rice and sweet potatoes. In other words, it's isolated.

Once inside, we are ushered to a room on the second floor for a PowerPoint presentation. I note that there doesn't seem to be a way for wheelchair users to get to this room. There's no elevator in evidence here, only stairs.

I learn that Lemon House supports adults with disabilities working in the community. Some are placed in a noodle restaurant, others take care of simple tasks in a dry cleaning business. Intellectually challenged individuals are also put to work in bakeries, in bento factories, and in a glass-making factory, where they make jewelry and other trinkets of brightly colored glass.

After the presentation, we peek into a resident's room downstairs, which is about the size of a business hotel room, and then go through large halls where workers make boxes or stuff envelopes or perform other simple tasks under the watch of an able-bodied supervisor. Some, for example those with autism who'd rather avoid the company of others, work behind screens fashioned out of cardboard. Others sort and assemble at tables, with company. They look up curiously as we pass through.

We also visit a small house that has been constructed nearby as a trial for independent living. Currently, and as for as long as they wish, two guys with autism are living there, with a rotating staff of helpers.

"It's not going as well as we hoped," our tour guide tells us. "The roommates don't get along, so their schedules are completely separate." Their possessions are strictly divided. There are two rolls of toilet paper in the bathroom, labeled with the owners' names. Apparently, aside from meal times, when they are in the house, they disappear behind the doors of their rooms where they don't have to deal with each other.

I'm impressed by the guide's honesty, and also cheered by the house. It's small, but there is nothing institutional about it. Maybe in ten years, Lilia could experiment in living in such a house herself. With a roommate. Or maybe someday with a husband! The rent would be just about covered by the monthly stipend she gets from the government. However, when I hear the wages for the workers in the on-site facility—200 yen (about $2) per hour, well below minimum wage—I wonder how Lilia will ever be able to save up enough money to travel to Paris.

On the mini-bus ride to visit another group home administered by Lemon House, I chat with Lilia's sixth grade teacher. I tell her about how and why I want my daughter to learn English and social studies and art, about how I don't think it's necessary to start preparing for a menial job in seventh grade. How long would it take her to learn how to stuff an envelope, anyhow? Five minutes?

But her teacher reminds me that all junior high school students are encouraged to think about future employment. There's this new problem in Japanese society with young adults who don't want to work, who just hang out in their parents' houses after graduation, playing video games. The ministry of education dictates that all kids, differently-abled or not, work as interns for a spell even though they aren't legally old enough to hold jobs, and, in the current dismal economy, their future employment prospects don't look so good. It's important, her teacher says, to begin preparing Lilia for the future. *Now.*

Well, then, if there's not enough time for all the classes that I want her to have, I'll teach her at home. I can teach her basic English and ASL: names of animals, colors, verbs, greetings for every time of day. And the tutor I hired for her a few years ago is qualified to teach art. Or maybe she can learn to paint and draw in a class somewhere, on Saturdays. I can take her to museums. As for social studies, she's probably learned more about the world already from her trips to America than she would have from sitting at a desk, reading a textbook. We'll travel and she'll learn more.

"I'll take you to Paris," I tell Lilia, not thinking, for once, about accessibility or the size of our bank account. "Just you and I." I'll teach her about art and history and the beginnings of sign language. We'll eat French food and cruise the Seine and take an elevator up the Eiffel Tower.

"Paris, later," she signs. "First, I want to go to Disneyland."

The Sound and the Worry

IN LILIA'S FIRST PASSPORT PHOTO, issued seven months after she was born, she sports plump cheeks and a double chin. About an inch of soft, fluffy brown hair sprouts from her head, and her tiny mouth is done up in a prim bow. She looks straight at the camera, her eyebrows arched in surprise. In this picture, taken at six months, she is sitting on my lap. She couldn't hold herself up yet. We didn't know then that due to oxygen deprivation sometime around her birth or shortly thereafter, she suffered brain damage, which would affect her arms and legs, especially on the left side. She has cerebral palsy, not uncommon in preemies.

In order to get the passport photos taken, I pushed my infant twins in a double stroller to a nearby camera shop. I posed each child on my lap, and then I pushed them back home. Then I filled out all of the necessary forms, left the twins with their father, and got on a bus by myself to Osaka, on the neighboring island of Honshu. There I found my way to the American consulate, where I claimed U.S. citizenship for my Japan-born babies.

LILIA AND HER BROTHER, Jio, came into the world on May 30, 1999, fourteen weeks before their due date. They weighed in at 690 grams and 964 grams, respectively. As soon as they were born, they were whisked away to the NICU, intubated and inserted with IVs, and settled into Plexiglas isolettes. For the next few months, Yoshi and I could only see our children after disinfecting ourselves and donning sterile clothing. We could only hold our babies for minutes at a time.

Our son, Jio, was finally released from the hospital in August. Lilia came home in September, four months after her birth. Before we left the NICU, the ample-bellied young doctor told us that we should avoid bringing our babies to crowded places such as grocery stores, shopping malls, and playgroups until they were at least two years old. Travel to the U.S. to see my family, or anywhere else, was out of the question. The doctor warned us that because their lungs had not sufficiently developed, a common cold could quickly turn into bronchitis or pneumonia or worse. He mentioned the possibility of heart failure.

Until we brought her home, Lilia had never been outside the NICU. The world must have seemed strange and scary to her. Instead of all of those sweet-tongued nurses in pink smocks, there were hulking, honking metal monsters. She cried in the car on the way home. I sang to her until she fell asleep.

Yoshi bought a musical mobile, and little chairs that squeaked when tiny bottoms sat upon them. He bought a stereo system just for the nursery so that our children would grow brilliant from Bach and Mozart, so that they'd be able to do calculus in kindergarten. "Only classical music," he insisted.

Secretly, I played other kinds of music for them—madrigals, folk, the didgeridoo, whale songs. Sometimes, Hootie & the Blowfish or Lucinda Williams crooning about car wheels on a gravel road. With the babies in my arms, I danced around the room and reveled in their smiles. I had always been able to derive energy and solace from music, but my husband devoted his youth to baseball and claims that he doesn't have a favorite band. One afternoon, Lilia was crying and I put on some music.

The gentle tinkle of George Winston's piano filled the room, and she was instantly calmed.

Sometimes I loaded the babies into the double stroller for walks. Our house was near Awa no Sato, a tourist complex consisting of restaurants, a bean jam bun factory, preserved farmhouses, a traditional garden, and an art gallery overlooking a pond full of brightly colored koi. On some days, I pushed the stroller into the art gallery and tried to get Lilia and Jio to look at the tapestries dyed with locally-grown indigo. On other days, we toured the bean jam bun factory, sampling the day's confection at the end, or lingered along the pond. When our shadows fell across the water, the fish surged en masse to the surface, expecting to be fed. The babies pointed in delight.

On an early winter evening, I was taking a shower and I felt a small bump in my left armpit. I felt it and my thoughts skidded over it—a follicle irritated by shaving; but later, when my mind went back, a lump under the arm. My mother's cousin, who had no family history of breast cancer, found a lump that proved to be malignant.

I touched it again the next morning. I thought about my children, imagined them without a mother. The next day, the protrusion was still there. I emailed my husband about it.

That night, he asked me about the lump. I told him that maybe it was nothing. I let him touch it.

"We are very happy," he said. "It's human nature to expect something bad to happen when everything is going too well."

He must be right, I thought, when the lump disappeared a day or two later. We had come through this huge drama with two healthy babies. They gurgled and cooed and beamed smiles into our faces. We had two children—exactly the right number—and what's more, we got a boy and a girl. How could we be so lucky?

WHEN WE BROUGHT LILIA to the pediatrician for a check-up, Yoshi said, "I don't think she can hear."

"But she stopped crying when I put on a CD," I argued. I

recalled how, another time, a music box had soothed her in the NICU. Even my mother-in-law who had been coming over to our house every day to help out was sure that Lilia could hear.

My husband was not convinced.

"Why don't we test her?" The doctor set up an appointment for an ABR (auditory brain stem response test).

A couple weeks later, she was sedated and electrodes were taped to her forehead. Earphones were fitted over her head. A machine produced bleeps of up to 100 decibels, but my daughter's brain waves exhibited no response.

So this is it, I thought. This is the calamity that I was expecting.

When I got home from the hospital, I cranked up the blues. The music was too loud for babies—for hearing babies, that is—but Lilia was oblivious. She stared at her hand, a starfish swimming in the light. She didn't move or even blink when I called out her name.

I spent the afternoon sobbing. How would I communicate with my daughter? What kind of relationship would we have? I didn't know anything about deafness. I had heard of Heather Whitestone, the first non-hearing Miss America, and I'd seen *Children of a Lesser God*, starring Marlee Matlin, but I'd never known an ordinary deaf person: a clerk, say, or a housewife. The only deaf person I could recall meeting was a girl in the fifth grade class at the school where I'd taught English as a foreign language. Because I had been teaching the other kids for five years already and she was new on the scene, and because I wasn't sure how much she could comprehend, I was hesitant to call upon her. I knew virtually nothing about deafness or deaf culture. I had no idea of what was in store for Lilia, or for our family. How would we cope with a deaf child? This was the kind of thing that would change our lives.

We would never be able to engage in girl talk, I thought, irrationally. We wouldn't be able to go to Paris.

I TOOK LILIA to the hospital for more tests. The young woman doctor who examined her told me that the results might not be entirely accurate as Lilia's cognitive development wasn't complete. The doctor said that in some cases, a child who exhibited no response as an infant might be tested again at age three and turn out to have normal hearing. But without sound, a child's brain will not develop normally. If she can't hear anything at all, her intellectual growth may be affected.

We were referred to the Tokushima School for the Deaf, which served the entire prefecture. My daughter was fitted with a hearing aid and we scheduled early intervention training sessions starting in the fall.

I called my family in South Carolina. My mother cried. I called my brother, father of a healthy toddler, and told him that I was grieving. "We're grieving too," he said. "But blind would have been worse." I wasn't sure that I could agree, but I understood that I had my family's love and support.

I was most concerned about my mother-in-law's reaction. A foreign daughter-in-law was bad enough. What would she make of a disabled granddaughter? On the other hand, by this time, she had been rocking and feeding and changing Lilia for months now. Surely, they had formed some sort of bond.

"She can have an operation later," my mother-in-law said. I wasn't sure what she was talking about, but at least she wasn't turning away.

A few days later, she said that we needed to inform the relatives before rumors got started. She mentioned a scandal concerning a dairy company that had been in the news that week. Something about tainted milk. I wonder what the hell that had to do with our family.

Of course shame about disability is not limited to Japan. There are many stories about parents who institutionalized their children on the advice of medical professionals, never to visit them again. Some of the parents became famous, or were famous already. Think Arthur Miller, who never bothered to mention his son who had Down Syndrome in his autobiography, or Pearl S. Buck, who kept her mentally challenged daughter's existence a secret for a long time.

Attitudes are changing in the United States, but Japan is a deeply conservative country, where one of the worst things you can do is to create a burden for someone else (someone outside the family, that is). One of my friends told me that she and her husband never barbecued outdoors because the odor would drift over to the neighbors' house, thus imposing upon others. In this country, it's best to make yourself as unnoticeable as possible. Don't make noise, don't dress conspicuously, don't disturb the harmony. *The nail that sticks up gets hammered down.*

The Japanese mothers at the deaf school talked about how people stared when their deaf children made weird, animal noises in public. Another mother worried that her hearing daughter wouldn't be able to get married. Maybe a prospective groom's family would worry about bad genes, or the future responsibility of looking after a sibling with disabilities. Marriage in Japan is a practical arrangement.

IT WAS HARD TO TELL how well Lilia could hear with amplification. In the beginning, she yanked out the hearing aids almost as soon as I put them on her ears. She hated them. They probably felt strange, nestled in the whorls of her ears. Even with the hearing aids, however, she didn't respond to voices or banged pots. Everyone told us that it would take time.

The teachers told me that I should help Lilia learn to listen by drawing her attention to sounds.

"Hey, hear that?" I asked. "That's the bread maker." I took her to the machine and let her feel the vibrations and watch the mixing of the dough.

"Listen!" I commanded, as a jet zoomed over our house, making its descent to land at the airport only a few miles away. I pointed to the sky and made the sign for airplane.

The doctors and teachers and books also instructed me to speak to Lilia as much as possible.

I spoke to her in English. The teachers told me that I should use only Japanese. They had little experience with bilingual families, or at least with mothers who aspired to raise their children bilingually. I later discovered that there were two other bicultural kids among the forty-plus students at the school: the daughter of a Filipina mother and Japanese father, and the daughter of a Brazilian mother of Japanese descent and her Japanese husband. As far as I could tell, the others had followed the teachers' instructions without question, but I wanted to try using English.

I brought them anecdotes from books and websites. about a Russian girl in New York City, for instance, that I'd read about in Leah Hager Cohen's book *Train Go Sorry*. This girl spoke two languages in addition to signing. The Japanese teachers were unconvinced. "It's too difficult for your daughter," they said.

When I married my husband, I knew he would never leave this country. As the oldest child and only son, he was responsible for his widowed mother. Plus, he loved his job as a high school teacher and baseball coach, and he was employed for life. He'd heard stories about my friends and family members in America who'd been laid off more than once. Why would he want to give up security, especially now that we had kids? He had never lived abroad, or even thought about it seriously. I was the one who wanted to try out another culture.

But I couldn't help thinking that Lilia would be better off in the United States. I had fantasies of her going to Gallaudet, the Washington D.C. College for the Deaf, and becoming a doctor or a lawyer. In Japan, deaf individuals were often steered toward careers in barber shops and beauty salons. There was a vocational program in hair-cutting at the Tokushima School for the Deaf.

In the meantime, it was too dangerous for us to travel. Airports were full of germs. A trip to my home country would be an unacceptable risk. So I bombarded Lilia with my language, preparing her for entry into the world.

YOSHI AND I began reading up on deafness, he in Japanese, me in English. I ordered a couple of videos and mastered the alphabet in American Sign Language. I started signing with both of our babies. I read up on cochlear implants.

I'd never heard of this new technology before, but the possibilities excited me at first. I told Yoshi about what I'd discovered: a flap of skin behind the ear is cut open, and electrodes are placed in the otherwise useless cochlea. A speech processor worn outside the body sends electronic impulses to the electrodes inside, which are then conveyed to the brain. This enables profoundly deaf individuals to hear a simulation of speech. Most deaf people can hear only a limited range of sounds, and a hearing aid can only amplify those sounds; but with a cochlear implant, a deaf person can have access to a wide range of sounds, from the low frequency of a boom of thunder, to the high frequency of whistling.

At first, Yoshi was skeptical. This operation was not widely performed in Japan at the time. Only one child in Tokushima had been implanted, and the jury was still out on the results.

KIMIKO NAGAO, the head of the early intervention program at the deaf school, was a competent and committed teacher. She was registered as a simultaneous interpreter of Japanese Sign Language and has many disabled friends. She knew about laws concerning the deaf in Sweden, about the latest happenings at Gallaudet University, and she had seen the deaf percussionist Evelyn Glennie in concert. She also seemed to be against cochlear implants and believed that Lilia could hear well enough with just a hearing aid.

She also recommended that I use only Japanese with Lilia, saying that it would be too difficult for a deaf child to master two spoken languages at once. Although I wasn't convinced of this, I did believe that it was important to use the same language all the time with my children. Switching from English to Japanese and back again would only confuse them. Until then, I'd used only English along with some American Sign

Language, at home. But now I would be accompanying my daughter to her early intervention sessions, and speaking Japanese to her teachers in her presence, and I would have to review and reinforce the Japanese she learned at the school. I suppose I could have refused, but I didn't feel qualified to take on her education all by myself. I needed outside support. I also knew that we would be living in Japan for a long time, and that my daughter needed to learn how to function in this country. I started speaking to Lilia in Japanese, but I continued to use only English with my son.

AT THE BEGINNING OF SEPTEMBER, I attended my first meeting of the Koala Club, a support group for the mothers of the one- to three-year-olds who attended the early intervention sessions at the School for the Deaf. There were seventeen mothers in all, but not everyone was in attendance. Two or three of us were new. There was another mother of twins, and a young woman with dyed blonde hair, now five months pregnant, who also gave birth to twins at twenty-six weeks. Only the boy survived, and apparently became deaf after birth.

The mothers talked about their month-long summer vacation while the teachers moderated. One told about her three-year-old daughter's operation, in which she received a cochlear implant. The girl was shy and clingy. She sometimes communicated with her mother via signs. Apparently, the mother was disappointed that the results had not been immediate and dramatic. She was not altogether sure that her daughter could hear, though the girl sometimes widened her eyes in response to sound.

There was another little girl whose hearing aids were connected by a yellow cord to keep them from getting lost, like mittens on a string. It seemed as if all of our children tended to take off their hearing aids. This little girl scribbled on the blackboard while loudly saying, "Wa wa wa wa."

Her mother greeted my daughter. She moved her flat hand over Lilia's head as if she were polishing an invisible halo. "*Yoi ko*," she said. "Good child."

BECAUSE OF MY FORMER CAREER in TEFL, and because I was hoping that my daughter would learn my language, I was interested in visiting English classes at the School for the Deaf.

I made arrangements to sit in on two junior high school English classes. In the first, there were usually two students, but one was absent. Keiko, the attendee, was a good-natured girl with long limbs and glasses. She pretended to be embarrassed by the prospect of two teachers at once, but gamely embarked upon the lesson.

On this day, the teacher and student played at shopping. Keiko ordered things—eggs, cheese, milk—from a list. I could just about understand her pronunciation, though comprehension would have been difficult if Keiko hadn't been pointing at pictures. When she finished "shopping," she counted out construction paper money to pay for her purchases.

"She can do math," the English teacher told me. "Fifty percent of the students here can't do basic calculations."

Would Lilia be able to count to one hundred, fifty, even ten one day? Would she be able to add and subtract? And if she couldn't, how would she get by?

In the second class, I met Chie. Although Chie had the black hair common to most Japanese, her eyes were an impossible cornflower blue. I wondered for a second if she wore contact lenses, but then the teacher said, "Look! Our visitor has eyes like yours!" I realized that the girl had probably been teased all of her life. I later discovered that blue eyes in Japanese often indicate a genetic aberration paired with deafness.

Before Chie stumbled late into class, the English teacher told me that her pronunciation would be difficult to understand. Now, as I listened to her read aloud a passage from her textbook, I found the words utterly incomprehensible.

For years, this school discouraged the use of sign language and pushed lip reading and vocalization. It was clear, however, that not everyone mastered speech. I didn't know how Chie would be able to communicate in the wider world outside this school, away from this kind and patient teacher who at least pretended to understand her.

THE FEATURED SPEAKER at the next Koala Club meeting was Ms. Onishi, the sole deaf teacher at the School for the Deaf. She was slender and attractive, in her thirties, with a flashy silver hearing aid. When she spoke, I understood her completely, and she in turn comprehended my American-accented Japanese. At last, a role model for Lilia, I thought. I figured she must have a husband and kids, and I wondered if they could hear. She was asked to talk to us about her experiences as a deaf person.

She told us, in clear Japanese, that her deafness was not discovered until she was in the fifth grade. During the preceding years, she had realized that she was different from others and wanted only to be understood. Instead, she was relentlessly bullied. On the way home from school, kids ripped the rucksack from her back and threw it in the bushes. She had memories of searching for her books with her parents in the night.

Many of us were moved to tears by this portrait of adolescent misery. I was amazed that she had functioned well enough to pass for a hearing person, albeit an odd and disobedient one. All those years of reading lips, of paying attention.

And now she had a job, a bright disposition, a normal life with e-mail and travel to foreign countries.

"I enjoy living by myself," she told us.

Of course, we'd all been wondering if she was married, worrying about our own children's prospects.

I didn't believe, as many Japanese women, that marriage was essential for happiness. Even so, I hoped that my daughter would one day experience falling in love and that she would be loved in return.

Someone asked Ms. Onishi if she wanted to marry.

"Yes," she replied. "If I have the chance."

Her response broke my heart. In this provincial Japanese

town, the odds of a thirty-something deaf woman finding a partner didn't seem good.

IN JANUARY, at the beginning of the new millennium, the Koala Club met again. The teachers handed out pieces of paper and asked us mothers to write our wishes for our children's futures.

In all honesty, I wanted my daughter to learn how to speak as well as a hearing person. I wanted her to have a "normal" life with marriage and kids and a job, although ultimately she might not want those things for herself. I wanted her to have options, however.

My wishes for her seemed a form of prejudice. By this time, I'd done some reading. I knew that there were many deaf people who had no desire to speak or hear, who were perfectly eloquent in sign language and comfortable in a culture of their own. I thought that I needed to pry my heart open wider.

I took out my pen and wrote that I wanted her to be happy.

"Is that all?" the teacher asked me.

Happiness is quite a lot, I thought, and not so easily attained. Even so, I thought some more and wrote "curiosity" and "the confidence to try whatever she wants to do."

I read over my words once or twice then handed the paper to the teacher.

BECAUSE OF THEIR DELICATE CONDITION, it would be many months before Lilia and Jio would actually use their passports. We kept the twins secluded at home, venturing out for walks, but not to playgroups or any other place where we might encounter other mothers and children and their germs. The twins ate, they slept, they grew. My son began to toddle. My daughter scooted around in a walker. Although Lilia's development was slower than Jio's, I wasn't particularly worried. After all, the NICU doctor had often said, "Don't worry!" Even later, during check-ups, when we were concerned about the way that her eyes seemed to cross, and over the fact that she had yet to learn to crawl, he assured us, “Don’t worry! She will advance little by little!” Such is the way of micro-preemies, he seemed to be saying. And I was reassured. For a bit. After all, I was still coming to terms with my daughter’s deafness. “Multiply-disabled” would take more getting used to.

Lilia had been getting physical therapy at the deaf school, but no one had offered any sort of diagnosis. Then one day, the school received a special visit from a hotshot therapist. He offered to take a look at Lilia.

“CP, right?” he said.

“What?”

“She has cerebral palsy?”

“No!” I was deeply offended. I didn’t even know exactly what cerebral palsy was, just that it sounded awful and debilitating. “She was extremely premature,” I explained to the specialist.

Okay, so maybe I was in denial.

Challenges

WE FINALLY BROKE OUT the passports to spend Christmas with my family in South Carolina. The twins, kept safely at home, except for visits to the School for the Deaf, hadn't been sick. They'd grown and developed. We figured we could get in one trip with our babies before we had to start paying for airfare for them. They were still small enough to hold on our laps, or to lay to sleep in the fold-down bassinets in bulkhead seating. They slept almost all the way to the United States.

In South Carolina, we visited Riverbanks Zoo, hung out with relatives, and gorged ourselves on turkey and stuffing. Jio ran around with his cousin, wrestling him to the floor, and getting into everything. Lilia dragged herself over the carpet with one arm: the combat crawl. Her head still wobbled a bit.

During that trip, my father, observing Lilia, said, "There's something wrong with her. You'd better get her checked out."

Back in Japan, Yoshi bought another book, one with pictures of children with pointed toes and curled hands. We took Lilia to Hinomine, a center for the education and care of physically disabled children. After an examination lasting only several minutes, the doctor scribbled, "suspected cerebral palsy," and prescribed therapy twice a week.

During the first session, I asked Mrs. Takubi, my daughter's new physical therapist, what the chances of her being able to walk one day were.

"It depends," Mrs. Takubi said, "upon her motivation, among other things. But I'd say 80%."

I nodded, satisfied. I figured she'd be walking in a year or so. We could put off our next trip abroad until she could get around on her own two feet. "So do you think she'll be walking by the time she's four?" I asked.

Mrs. Takubi made a stalling noise.

Okay, I thought. So maybe four-and-a-half.

And then Lilia caught a cold.

A COUPLE OF MONTHS before her second birthday, my daughter was hospitalized for bronchitis. Her lungs were still weak. Over the next two years, she was in and out of the hospital ten times for respiratory ailments. On the first day, she'd have the tiniest trickle of snot coming out of her nose. Twenty-four hours later, she would be in the ICU, intubated and sedated, hooked up to a respirator, sometimes fighting for her life. Each hospital stay was a setback. She would lose weight, and muscle tone. If, before she became ill, she could stand by grabbing onto a railing, she'd emerge from the ICU weak and unable to hold herself upright. For about a year, she seemed to make no progress at all.

On the rare occasions when we could make it to the School for the Deaf (when the weather was warm, when Lilia was healthy), she was given hearing tests. One May morning, shortly after recovering from a bout with pneumonia, she scored in the 50-60 decibel range. This indicated that she was only mildly to moderately deaf.

"She could almost do without a hearing aid," I said, trying to contain my joy.

The teacher who had administered the test gave me a wry smile. "Well, not exactly."

When I told my husband about the test results, he was unimpressed. At home, we'd never seen her respond to sound.

He had been pushing for a cochlear implant ever since we saw a documentary on educational television.

"But Nagao-sensei says that she can hear at 50 decibels with a hearing aid," I insisted.

Yoshi snorted. "I don't think so." He yelled at our daughter, sitting there in her high chair, to demonstrate. "Lilia!"

She didn't look, didn't even move her head.

"Nagao-sensei is just trying to make the parents feel better. She's telling you what you want to hear."

I rolled my eyes. This was a man who believed the Oliver Stone version of JFK's assassination, who thought that maybe George W. Bush was complicit in 9/11.

"Nagao-sensei wants to protect deaf culture."

I disagreed, but the point was moot. Either way, she wasn't yet healthy enough to have a major operation.

WHILE I KNEW THAT the first girl at the School for the Deaf to receive a cochlear implant had made rapid progress since summer and that the results of her operation were better than anyone had expected, none of the teachers at the school had encouraged us to make the same decision for Lilia. In fact, many of them seemed to know very little about cochlear implants in general. Some were skeptical. One suggested that Lilia had not developed orally because I spoke to her in English, while everyone around us used Japanese. Meanwhile, other children in Lilia's age group began to say "mama" and "bye bye."

While I believed that a cochlear implant might help her, I couldn't bear the thought of putting Lilia in the hospital again. I didn't think I could stand to see another needle shoved into her vein, another tube jammed down her throat, another IV dripping overhead. And I didn't want anyone cutting anywhere near my daughter's beautiful head. If she could hear at 50 decibels, she could hear speech. A cochlear implant would be unnecessary, almost a crime, I thought.

From time to time I checked the audiograph of Lilia's latest hearing test, but as summer vacation dragged along, I began to have doubts. No matter how many times I called out Lilia's name, she never turned her head. One day, while I was driving, she fell asleep in the car. As soon as she shut her eyes, I turned the radio way up. It was so loud that the car was vibrating and my own ears throbbed with pain. Although Lilia's sleep was still shallow, she didn't wake up.

Meanwhile, she had made progress with sign language. When she wanted something to drink, she tilted her thumb toward her mouth. She scrunched her fingers together in the sign for "ouch." At dinnertime, if she wanted more meat, she pinched the skin on the back of her hand. I was learning along with her, but I was far from fluent. Lilia could only communicate with a few people, and I feared that without a constant bombardment of language, her linguistic development was hampered.

Subsequent hearing test results were not so good. Her scores fell into the severe to profound range. Finally, an ear/nose/throat specialist who'd tested her several times in the past asked if she'd ever been given steroids.

"Yes," I said. "Every time she was in the hospital. For her lungs."

A mystery was solved. It was determined that the steroids temporarily improved her hearing. When the effects wore off, her ability to hear declined. The specialist suggested a regular schedule of steroids.

We were horrified. So was her pediatrician, the doctor who'd looked after her for four months in the NICU and beyond. We were working to wean Lilia off all medication. Steroids would affect her whole body.

When we expressed out feelings to the specialist, he conceded that Lilia might benefit from a cochlear implant.

IN RETROSPECT, traveling at that time wasn't such a good idea, but I needed to get out of Japan. I needed to see my family. I decided to take the twins back to South Carolina for the summer. I booked a house on the Atlantic coast, thinking I'd fulfill my dream of a beach vacation, deposit non-refundable. And then my daughter got sick again. Luckily, with a doctor's note, I was able to get back the money I'd paid for plane tickets. The beach house apparently remained empty for a week.

In October, I tried again. My husband stayed behind, and I managed to get my three-year-olds from Tokushima to Tokyo, where we met up with a writer friend who lived on a farm with chickens and cats, then onward to San Francisco, where we stayed for a couple days with another writer friend. Then we went on to South Carolina, where my daughter got sick again. She was diagnosed with pneumonia, given some medication and sent home, or at least to my parent's house.

By this time, she was strong enough to stay out of the hospital. I left her behind while I took my son to the State Fair where we saw a backhoe rodeo and prize-winning cows. We rode on the Tilt-A-Whirl. Lilia was healthy enough to play in the sandbox and dig out the guts of the pumpkin that my dad carved for Halloween.

On our way back to Japan, we were supposed to stay with one of my old Tokushima friends in San Francisco, but she herself had just given birth prematurely. It didn't seem like a good idea to have a kid recovering from a respiratory ailment in the house with an underweight newborn baby. We stayed with her parents. Her father just happened to be a pediatrician, and I asked him what he thought about my daughter, who was such a poor eater, who'd get food caught in her throat and start coughing and throw up, who never seemed to gain enough weight. He thought a tonsillectomy might be a good idea.

When we got back to Japan, Lilia had a tonsillectomy, spent a couple days recuperating in the ICU due to respiratory-related complications, and then she finally began to grow. Tests revealed that Lilia was indeed profoundly deaf. At her healthiest, even with hearing aids, she could hear almost nothing at all.

Once again, Yoshi and I began to discuss the possibility of an implant for our daughter. We knew that it wouldn't cure her deafness, but it if were successful, the operation would provide access to the spoken word. If she could hear what we were saying, she might be able to learn to speak herself. This was starting to seem a lot better than the sink-or-swim system of deaf education in Japan where, no matter how intelligent a child is, only the best lip-readers go on to college and professional careers.

In the United States at this time, a cochlear implant for a deaf child was a controversial choice. One of the arguments against this relatively safe operation was that it threatened Deaf culture. Here in Japan, where deaf children were frequently mainstreamed and might very well grow up having little or no contact with their deaf peers, there was no deaf culture to speak of.

Japan didn't even have a standard form of sign language. And while many schools and universities had sign language clubs, JSL wasn't offered as an academic course as it was in American schools. Even at the Tokushima School for the Deaf, the signs taught in the early intervention program were different from the signs taught on Japan's publicly supported educational TV station, or even different from the signs taught in the junior high school. Signs varied from generation to generation as well as from region to region. I'd also figured out by now that the teachers at the deaf school weren't really using JSL, with its particular rules of grammar, but were signing Japanese as it would normally be written or spoken. There was also a heavy emphasis on fingerspelling, which can be very tedious to follow, but which would help students to become literate in Japanese.

My own remaining reservations about a cochlear implant had to do with a fear of the unknown. Cochlear implants were relatively new in 2000. They had been approved by the U.S. Food and Drug Administration less than twenty years before. In a brochure provided by the manufacturer, I read, "The long-term effects of electrode insertion trauma or chronic electrical stimulation are unknown." Hardly comforting words. But I was beginning to think that this was Lilia's one big chance. I wanted her to have every advantage that we could give her, and I reasoned that if something went seriously wrong, the implant could be removed.

After a CT-scan and X-rays at a hospital in Matsuyama, a city on the other side of the island of Shikoku famous for its tangerines, our daughter was proclaimed to be a good candidate for the procedure. We made a decision.

The afternoon before surgery, my husband took Lilia to a beauty salon on the first floor of the hospital. The beautician shaved a curved path over her right ear. The following morning, her father carried her to the operating theater. Lilia waved cheerily as he made his exit.

The operation lasted six hours. When I next saw Lilia, she was no longer cheerful. A huge wad of gauze was taped to the side of her head. She was in pain and she was angry.

How could I explain that this operation was a gift? That we were providing her with sound, expanding her future possibilities? Neither the coloring book provided by the hospital nor the teddy bear with the toy speech processor and magnet had prepared her for the pain.

I sat by her hospital bed for the next few days. We didn't know anybody in Matsuyama. No one came to visit us. Her father had gone back across the island to work, and her twin brother was staying with his aunt, so it was just the two of us. "Moon River" blared from the town hall every evening at 6PM. Soon, when the swelling went down and she was hooked up to the speech processor, Lilia would be able to hear it, too.

THE DAY BEFORE LILIA got sound, I asked Yoshi what he expected her reaction would be like. He acted it out: wonder blossoming into joy.

I had braced myself for a total lack of response. According to the *Parent's Guide: A Handbook for Parents Considering a Nucleus*

Cochlear Implant for Their Child, initial reactions to sound ranged from "no reaction at all" to "surprisingly matter-of-fact" and from "sheer delight" to "absolute terror." I tried to hold my expectations in check, but I was excited all the same.

We arrived at the hospital the following evening. It was after hours and the second floor was deserted and dark, except for the sofa where a female graduate student awaited us. She assured us that Dr. Takahashi, the audiologist who would oversee Lilia's habilitation, would be along shortly.

He bustled in with a computer, a bag of toys, and another graduate student and led us into a carpeted room. The young doctors who had assisted at Lilia's operation were called in as well.

Dr. Takahashi was present during the insertion of the electrodes. Now, he explained each step of sound input to the physicians. He affixed the magnetic coil, which would transmit electrical signals to Lilia's brain, to the side of her head. He hooked the microphone over her ear and connected it to the speech processor, a device about the size of a cellphone. The speech processor was connected to his computer. And then he gave Lilia sound.

By the look on her face, I knew she'd heard something. This was the look she got when she saw a smear of mud on her leg, or when a crab got too close. This furrowed brow face told me that she heard something and she didn't like it.

Over the next hour, she removed the coil and microphone several times and tried to return the apparatus to Dr. Takahashi: Thanks, but no thanks. Her response wasn't exactly what we'd hoped for, but it was encouraging all the same. *She could hear.*

Back home, I sat by the window and listened. Frogs croaked. Insects chirred and buzzed. I could hear the man in the house behind ours coughing up phlegm, cars whooshing along Highway 11, a neighbor's telephone ringing. Sirens, the soughing of wind, cats in heat.

The world was noisy, and Lilia would find the ability to

hear a mixed blessing. Although she would learn to use her hearing, she would continue to prefer communicating via sign language.

Deaf in D.C.

OF COURSE, Lilia wanted to go to Disneyland. She'd been born into the Culture of Cute, where the image of Mickey (so well-known that here in Japan he goes by first name only, much like Ichiro and Madonna) proliferates without a trace of irony. The birth of Lilia and Jio brought on a barrage of Disney-branded goods. We were given Minnie and Mickey blankets, chairs, clothing, futon covers, dishes, stuffed dolls, push toys, bath towels and a music box that played the theme to "The Mickey Mouse Club." Most extravagant of all was the triple-tiered crib mobile with dangling pink blossoms and a plastic baby Mickey. Throughout kindergarten, Lilia and her classmates had held monthly birthday celebrations. The cakes were decorated with the kids' favorite cartoon characters, which were often one of the Disney princesses. It was inevitable that whenever she saw a commercial for Disneyland on TV, she signed "*Ikkitai!*"

"When you're ten," I promised. But the winter that Jio and Lilia turned ten, Yoshi and I planned a family trip not to Tokyo, but to the United States. In addition to maintaining family ties and giving Jio a chance to improve his English, traveling to the States was a way to help our kids understand that there was life beyond our safe, but conservative small town where they were sometimes called "*gaijin*" (foreigner) or "*hafu*" (half). I also wanted to nurture Jio and Lilia's American side. They had dual citizenship, after all. According to Japanese law, they would have to choose a single nationality when they were twenty. An American passport wasn't easy to come by. I wanted them to have some idea of what it meant.

After spending Christmas with my family, we flew to Washington D.C. to visit our friend Bill, who was the reason Yoshi and I were together at all.

I first met Bill, with his curly dark hair and beard, on my second day in Japan. He and I were both on the JET (Japan Exchange and Teaching) Program sponsored by the Japanese Ministry of Education. The idea was to employ spirited young native English speakers to assist in teaching language in Japanese public junior and senior high schools. Japanese ability wasn't necessary, but during the orientation speeches, Bill whiled away the time by practicing writing kanji. He'd studied Japanese at college and was well on his way to fluency. Bill, ten others and I were sent to Tokushima Prefecture on the island of Shikoku where there was no high-speed bullet train and few Westerners.

Both Bill and I decided to stay on for a second year. I hadn't yet climbed Mt. Fuji as I'd planned or bought a string of real pearls (also on the list), or seen much of Asia. I wasn't sure when I'd ever come back, so I wanted to experience as much as I could while I had the chance. A couple of months into my second year as an Assistant Language Teacher, Bill's parents came to visit him. He arranged a party at a restaurant in Tokushima City for them, inviting the friends he'd made in Japan.

Bill's colleague and weight-lifting partner, a handsome young Japanese P.E. teacher in a pink polo shirt, sat across the table from me. "Do you speak Japanese?" he asked.

"*Sukoshi,*" I said. A little.

He seemed to give up on conversation, but later he offered to give me a ride home. The side window of his car had been taped up after a student at the night school where he worked had shattered it with a baseball bat. New teachers were often sent to the toughest schools for their first positions, which seemed to me like a kind of hazing, then later rewarded with quiet, obedient, academically minded students.

Yoshi dropped me off. The next day, he told Bill that he thought I was pretty. I admitted that I wouldn't mind getting to know him better. He wasn't the dumb jock I'd expected, but had turned out to be thoughtful and intelligent, and man enough to wear a pink shirt. Plus, he hadn't been freaked out by my foreignness, as many Japanese people were back then.

Bill arranged for us to go on a double-date, so a week later, Bill, Yoshi, my friend Rumi and I played mini golf together then went out for drinks and karaoke. Using a dictionary, we managed to communicate in a combination of English and Japanese and got to know each other better. Four years later, Bill attended our wedding in Hawaii.

Now Bill was earning a living as a freelance interpreter. He'd started out working for the State Department, interpreting for the likes of Hillary Clinton and Shinzo Abe. He'd flown on Air Force One and been in the same room as Colin Powell. Though currently based in Washington D.C., he often traveled to gigs in far off places such as Qatar, for an international sporting event, and Japan. Jio, who had developed a keen interest in politics, was duly impressed.

Bill picked us up at the airport in a rented car. He drove us past the embassies of many nations—India, Korea, Italy, etc.—to his apartment building. Jio was wowed by the rooms with a view.

"It's very...neat," I said, taking in the black leather sofa and the original art on the walls. The tables and counters were surprisingly clutter-free, the newspapers neatly stacked in a box. Bill had been rather messy in Japan.

"I have someone come in once a week," he admitted. "I'm still a slob."

Maybe it was right about then that Jio decided that he

wanted to be a professional interpreter when he grew up. Not only would he be able to travel and meet famous people, but also he'd make enough money to have someone else tidy up his messy room!

Bill had already seen the tourist attractions of the nation's capital, so the next day he made plans to work out at the gym and dropped us off at the Smithsonian Museum of Natural History, which Lilia recognized from the movie *Night Museum*. She posed for photos in front of the Easter Island Moais, the dinosaur bones, and the Hope diamond. Later, we posed in a variety of configurations in front of the White House.

"President Obama lives here," I reminded Lilia and Jio. They knew that he was biracial and bicultural, just as they were. Whatever their political views, most American expatriates in Japan were glad that a multicultural man occupied the White House. Born to a white mother and a Kenyan father and raised partly in Indonesia, he was a role model for Third Culture Kids everywhere.

I'd tried to book a tour of the White House, but it wasn't as easy as I'd expected. Although I sent an email to my congressman in South Carolina, there were no tours scheduled between Christmas and New Year's. We satisfied ourselves with gaping at the gate. A security officer gave Lilia a commemorative medallion. Nearby, a war protestor who'd lost his son was camped out on the pavement. According to his sign, he'd been there for over a year.

WE HAD A RESERVATION for a tour of the Capitol building the next morning. After borrowing an audio guide in Japanese for Yoshi, in the Capitol Visitor Center we took in the statues representing notable people from the history of various states. There was the golden-caped King Kamehameha I of Hawaii in bronze and North Dakota's Sacagawea, the Shoshone woman who'd famously served as an interpreter for the explorers Lewis and Clark. South Carolina had contributed a marble statue of Confederate cavalry leader, and later governor, Wade Hampton.

From across the room, Lilia beckoned to me.

"What?" I wagged my finger.

"Helen Keller!" Although the label was in English, she'd recognized the figure of a girl standing by a water pump. Keller was from Alabama.

"Her reputation has suffered some because of her communist leanings," a Visitor Center employee told me.

"She's still big in Japan," I said. The Kinokuniya bookstore near our house had half a dozen biographies of Helen in stock at any given time. She'd made two trips to Japan. On the first, in 1937, she delivered a letter on behalf of President Roosevelt, reconfirming friendship between nations. On the second, in 1948, she visited Hiroshima and Nagasaki and spoke against the atomic bomb. She even acquired a dog from Japan, an Akita named Kamikaze-Go, after being inspired by the statue of the faithful Hachiko at Shibuya Station.

"Would you like an ASL interpreter for your daughter?" the employee asked.

"Oh, that would be great! But she only knows Japanese Sign Language...."

"Maybe they're similar?"

I agreed that it was worth a try. She went to the front desk to inquire.

When the ASL interpreter, a middle-aged woman in a pantsuit, arrived, she introduced herself to Lilia via sign language. Lilia had no idea what she was communicating. In spite of what most people think, sign language is not universal. Signs vary even between English-speaking countries and are often culturally specific. Many Japanese signs, for example, are based upon written ideograms.

"Thanks for trying," I told the interpreter. "We'll go it on our own." I handed Lilia the camera. As the tour progressed, she took photos of the rotunda while I listened to our guide, collecting interesting facts to share with her later. I was surprised to learn, for example, that the life-sized statue of Abraham Lincoln in the rotunda had been sculpted after his death by Vinnie Ream, a young woman without any formal artistic training who'd won the coveted commission over several more experienced artists. When she was sixteen, she'd persuaded the president to sit for a bust. I also hadn't known that it was Abraham Lincoln who'd signed the charter for the first college for the deaf in the world: the National Deaf Mute College in Washington D.C., which is now called Gallaudet University.

After our tour, Yoshi wanted to check out the food court at Penn Station, which had been recommended by a Japanese tourist guide, so Bill picked us up and we went to get lunch. At the train station we found stairs leading to the first level where the restaurants were, but the elevator didn't descend. "Maybe we can't take the wheelchair down there," I said.

A twenty-something African-American man standing nearby overheard me. "Of course there's a way to get down," he piped up. "It's the law!"

We eventually found an elevator down a somewhat remote hall, behind some boxes, and nabbed a table in the busy food court.

Jio scarfed down his burger in record time. "I'm still hungry."

"Here's some money," I said, handing over a five. "Do you think you can order another hamburger by yourself?"

Bill shook his head. "You shouldn't let him wander around alone. It's not safe."

"Oh...right." After so many years of living in Japan, where crime was uncommon, and where even in Tokyo, elementary school kids walked to school without adult supervision, I'd forgotten about the dangers of urban America. I followed Jio through the crowd and queued up with him at the counter.

Our stomachs full, we moved on to the National Air and Space Museum. In the lobby, one of the legendary African-American Tuskegee Airmen was signing copies of his new book. The place was packed with visitors from all over the world. I could make out people speaking Spanish, Japanese and French.

Yoshi had wanted to see the Enola Gay, the plane from which the atomic bomb had been dropped on Hiroshima, but we found out that it was at a different branch of the museum in Virginia. Still, there was much to see: rockets, a space shuttle simulator, a copy of the Wright Brothers' airplane, and one of Amelia Earhart's planes.

"My great great grandmother," Lilia signed.

"Uh, no. That's a different Amelia," I told her. "My great grandmother was a teacher, not a pilot." I'd wanted to name my daughter "Amelia" after her, but Yoshi had thought it was too long, even though it was only one syllable longer than the name we finally decided upon. Nevertheless, Lilia liked the name, and was especially interested in anyone named Amelia. Later, when a manga biography of the famous flyer was published, I'd buy her a copy so she could know more about Earhart's extraordinary life. Lilia would swiftly add the aviator to her pantheon of heroines.

Bill wasn't much of a cook, so we stopped by Whole Foods on the way back to his apartment and Yoshi bought ingredients for a Japanese breakfast. Since giving up baseball, he had time to cultivate his inner chef and he now made dinner on weekends and breakfast for us at home. The next morning, Yoshi made miso soup while Lilia asked Bill questions by writing in Japanese: "What kind of animals do you like? What's your favorite fruit? What's your dream?"

Later that afternoon, Bill dropped us off at the Lincoln Memorial. The tour guide at the Capitol had mentioned the huge statue of the enthroned Abe in his spiel. "Take a look at the hands," he'd said. "Some people say they form the letters A and L, the president's initials." The creator of this statue, Daniel Chester French, had also sculpted Thomas H. Gallaudet, founder of the first school for the Deaf in America, and Alice Cogswell, who was the first American deaf pupil.

I pointed Lincoln's hands out to Lilia. "See? He's doing sign language." Back when Lilia was a baby, I'd mastered the ASL alphabet and I'd taught her how to fingerspell her name in English, so she recognized the letters.

From the steps of the memorial, we could see far, far over the heads of the many tourists from around the world, across the reflecting pool to the Washington Memorial, which shot like an arrow into the cloudless blue sky. Down below on the steps, a Yankees cap on his head, Jio practiced his pitching form. He'd started playing baseball on a team at a nearby elementary school, going from the worst player on the team to the one with the best batting average. In Japan, junior high school baseball is a year-round activity. Watching him, I realized that if he continued to play it would become harder and harder to bring him to America, or anywhere else for that matter. He wouldn't want to miss practice because if he did, he wouldn't be allowed to participate in games. This might be our last big family trip abroad for a while, I thought sadly.

After we'd regrouped, we walked across the street to a park to wait for Bill. We bought coffee and hot chocolate from the little kiosk and sat on the bench outside sipping and watching the squirrels scampering about. For Yoshi and the twins, the animals were exotic. I'd once seen a chipmunk in a pet shop in Japan, and ferrets inhabited the bushes near our house, but I'd never seen squirrels in the wild before on Shikoku.

While we were hanging out and chatting, a young woman approached us. "I saw you signing with your daughter," she said. "Is it okay if I talk to her?" She was studying ASL, she explained, and she wanted to try it out. "Go ahead," I offered. "But she knows mostly Japanese Sign Language."

Back in Tokushima, very few people seemed to know sign language. Although Japanese elementary school children were often taught a song or two in sign language, JSL didn't command the same level of respect as ASL. It was refreshing to find so many people eager to converse in sign with Lilia, even if it was a slightly different language.

I stood back observing as the young woman signed to Lilia.

"*Nani?*" Lilia wagged her finger and looked to me. *What?*

"She's studying American Sign Language," I signed to Lilia.

"She wants to say 'hello.'"

Lilia bowed to her. "*Arigatou.*" She made a chopping motion, the JSL sign for "thank you."

When Bill finally arrived, we piled into the rental car and set out for our last stop of the day, the statue commemorating the U.S. Army's WWII victory at Iwo Jima. It was one of the most harrowing battles for the Japanese. On the way, we glimpsed the Jefferson Memorial through the bare branches of cherry trees brought from Japan.

Disney and Disaster

ONE AFTERNOON IN March, 2011, while Lilia and Jio are at school, I'm home at my computer. I don't have any part-time university classes on this day, so I'm catching up on some writing assignments and checking Facebook updates. It's 2:26 PM.

"Whoa. Earthquake!" a friend in Osaka posts. Nothing unusual there. Japan is riddled with faults, and the ground shakes a lot. Other friends who live near Tokyo start chiming in: "Did you feel that one?" "Is everyone okay?" As usual.

I check the clock. Time to pick up Lilia. I close the computer window, get into my hatchback, and drive along the road in front of our house, which parallels the wide, once wild, Yoshino River. As I cross the bridge, I gaze out toward the Inland Sea, toward Kobe, which was struck by a devastating early morning earthquake in 1995. I remember how our fifth floor apartment had swayed, like bamboo in a breeze. I'd stood on the bed in terror, trying to remember what we were supposed to do. Open the door so we didn't get trapped in the rubble? Climb under the table so we didn't get crushed by falling debris? Run, run, run down the stairs? Yoshi, who'd spent four years in college near Tokyo, had experienced many tremors, and for him it was no big deal. He laughed at me. Thankfully, our building stayed intact, but over 5,000 people in Kobe were killed that day. I shake my head to clear the memory, then take the turn for the School for the Deaf.

I park at the side of the dirt playground and get out of the car. Lilia, in her wheelchair, and her home room teacher are already waiting for me. The principal, a large man with black-rimmed glasses and a shock of white hair, stands nearby. Normally, he stays in his office. Am I in trouble? The teachers sometimes scold me for bringing Lilia to school late, or for forgetting to sign permission slips. I walk slowly toward them.

"There's been an earthquake," the principal says in an urgent tone.

I nod. "I know."

"A big one." His brow furrows. "A tsunami warning has been issued for Tokushima. You need to hurry home."

A tsunami warning? Yikes. I know that years before, a giant wave washed over Tokushima's southern coast. Wooden houses were ripped apart by the force of the waters, boats overturned, and trees uprooted. Entire families drowned. Even now the descendants of survivors gather annually to float lighted candles on the sea and remember the dead.

Lilia, who has already been apprised of the risk, wheels herself vigorously to the car. She opens the door and heaves herself inside.

The principal tells me that the tsunami is due to arrive in another hour or so. I think that we have plenty of time to get home, but I gaze anxiously at the river as I drive. Has it risen? During a heavy rain the road often becomes flooded. If the water surges suddenly, we could be washed away, swept out to the river. Even if we managed to get out of the car, Lilia, weighted with heavy leg braces, wouldn't float.

We can see my son's school from the road. Kids in baseball uniforms are on the field as usual, with seemingly no sense of impending danger. Meanwhile, sirens blare along the riverbanks, warning people to seek higher ground. Our house is on the other side of the levee. I think that we are safe.

Once we reach our home, I quickly get Lilia inside and

turn on the television. I am immediately seized with horror. Shaky cell phone footage shows people scrambling up hills, voices imploring others to hurry, black water creeping forward like a liquid beast. I can't help thinking about how hard it would be to get a wheelchair up those inclines. Should we get back into the car and start driving toward the low mountains farther west? We see people standing on roofs, on the tops of cars, on a bridge that is about to be consumed by waves. We see houses topple and crash, floating cars, water clogged with debris. For the next hour or so, I switch between my computer and the television, frantic for information. My brother sends a panicked email from South Carolina, saying that he's heard a nuclear reactor in Tokushima has been damaged. I find a similar notice on the internet, but it's wrong, I assure him. There are no nuclear power plants in Tokushima Prefecture. Later, the news site corrects its report. The nuclear power plant in *Fukushima* has been damaged, leading to a meltdown. When Yoshi and Jio return home, our entire family remains glued to the television for hours.

The tsunami, when it arrives in Tokushima, is only a little over a meter high. As it turns out, the epicenter of the earthquake was in Miyagi Prefecture, about 500 miles away. We are physically safe, this time, but our hearts are aching. Elsewhere, there is chaos and unimaginable destruction. The earthquake measured 9 on the Moment magnitude scale making it the fourth largest earthquake ever recorded in history, triggering tsunami waves up to 40.5 meters high, and shifting the axis of the earth. In northern Japan and in Tokyo there are fires, fissures, and concerns about radioactivity.

In the aftermath, people are stranded at Tokyo Disneyland. We watch the coverage of the shaken tourists trapped in the Magic Kingdom from the safety of our living room in Shikoku. There are immediate concerns about aftershocks, liquefication (the theme park was built on a landfill), and then radiation. Once the park is evacuated, Disneyland is temporarily closed down.

Japan is arguably the most disaster-ready nation on earth. Earthquake drills are held regularly at my children's schools. Outside my daughter's classroom—and every other classroom - there is a backpack with emergency supplies. My kids, and every other kid in Japan, have padded, fireproof hoods near their desks. While drills had been held periodically before March 11, in the weeks after the disaster my daughter practices for earthquakes every day. Her teacher tells me that although at first she dawdled, she is getting faster at crawling under her desk. But her classroom is on the first floor of an old building that still bears cracks from the Great Hanshin Earthquake in 1995. If there is an actual earthquake of similar magnitude, she will likely be trapped and crushed by the upper floors, no matter how many earthquake drills she's endured.

The Japan Times begins publishing daily radiation reports. It's weird at first, then normal. According to the report on December 5, 2011, the town Iitate, near the damaged nuclear power plants in Fukushima, is exposed to 2.039 microsieverts of radiation per hour. In Chiba Prefecture, where Disneyland is located, the rate is .052 per hour, which is safe according to the government. Safe enough for a brief trip, we hope. Maybe we can finally take our daughter to Disneyland. We start to make plans.

Being a Japanese special ed teacher accustomed to students with autism who depend upon rigid schedules, Yoshi makes out a detailed itinerary for our trip and holds a family meeting to discuss it. For the record, it's nothing compared to the ten-page printout I'd once been handed by a PTA mother for a class cook-out, but I still find it impressively - maybe even *oppressively*- thorough.

According to the schedule, we will be leaving at 6AM on Christmas morning. Breakfast will be *onigiri* (rice balls). Lunch will be bentos and *udon* noodles at a rest stop, and dinner, *yakisoba* (fried noodles) cooked Shizuoka-style. We will travel 504 kilometers, stopping for the night at a hotel with a view of Mt. Fuji.

Seeing Mt. Fuji live, in person, will be another quintessential experience for our children. The sacred mountain is to Japan, what the Eiffel Tower is to France. One of my earliest and most enduring images of this country is a photo in the World Book encyclopedia of the bullet train speeding past the iconic peak. My own first real-life view of Fuji-san was from a Shinjuku hotel window on a clear day, just after I'd arrived in Japan. I've seen it several times since then—from airplane windows, from a park in Yokoyama, and once, up close, during a visit with my parents. Jio and Lilia have not yet had the pleasure.

Yoshi has also made a list of what we are supposed to bring along: a suitcase, long pants, toothbrushes and toothpaste, underwear, socks, neckwarmers, and knit caps, among other things. I get to choose CDs for our listening pleasure.

On Christmas morning, as planned, we pile our car with blankets and food—tuna sandwiches, bento-boxed lunches, Soy Joy bars, tangerines, and homemade banana bread—and set off. The sun is just bursting through the clouds, painting the sky pink and orange. Since it's a Sunday, there are few cars on the road. We've heard rumors of snow in Kyoto and its environs, but so far, the signs bode well. Although Mt. Fuji is often obscured by clouds, if the weather holds, we just might be able to catch a glimpse.

Lilia, in the backseat, tracks our progress on a road map. Her finger falls on Naruto as we cross the bridge connecting Shikoku to Awaji Island. Underneath, we see the white froth of the whirlpools churning the waters. After we cross the island with its many onion fields, and traverse another suspension bridge, we enter Kobe.

In the years since the Great Hanshin Earthquake, the city has been entirely rebuilt. Highways once again rise above the earth, winding through a hodgepodge of many-storied buildings. Glass and metal glimmer in the morning sunshine. Off to the right, we catch glimpses of the sea, and, as the city melds into Osaka, the colorful castle-like waste treatment center on

Majima. On the left, we see Koshien baseball stadium, home of the Hanshin Tigers, and site of the annual high school baseball tournament, the rollercoasters of Universal Studios Japan.

Outside the city limits, we go through numerous tunnels, and finally, farther north, catch sight of snow-frosted mountains. Tree-topped hills stretch into the distance. Flocks of clouds hover above. Beyond Hamamatsu, a city known for its large Brazilian immigrant population and its Honda factory, we begin to spot the tea fields of Shizuoka, some of them studded with small wind turbines. Deep pink *sazanka* blossoms decorate the bushes along the meridian.

And then, finally, "Fuji-san!" Yoshi cries.

Yes, there it is, looming unmistakably over the surrounding mountains, its peak dolloped with a fluffy white cloud. Surprisingly, there is no snow on the slopes.

"Waaaa!" Lilia exclaims.

Jio, in the front passenger seat, begins snapping pictures like a modern-day digital Hokusai. Lilia grabs her notebook and begins to draw a picture of the mountain. I just enjoy the view.

We keep driving. Before checking into our room-with-a-view, we must, according to the itinerary, have our dinner of Shizuoka-style fried noodles. Yoshi consults the car's navigation system for restaurants that specialize in yakisoba, noodles typically sautéed with thinly sliced pork and vegetables, and mixed with a rich brown sauce. Yakisoba is a staple of home cooking. The first noodle shop that we are directed to by the ever-placid voice doesn't have parking. The second is a tiny mom-and-pop business down a dark alley. The kids and I wait in the idling car while Yoshi goes to investigate. By now our stomachs are complaining loudly and the city is cloaked in darkness, but he shakes his head as he comes back to the car.

"It's too narrow for a wheelchair."

"Why don't we just go to Gusto?" I say, naming a chain restaurant we passed earlier. It doesn't have a lot of character, but it's reliable and barrier-free.

"How about McDonald's?" Jio asks.

Lilia signs that she's hungry. "*Tabetai*!"

"Shizuoka yakisoba won the B Gourmet Grand Prix!" Yoshi insists, referring to a competition celebrating street food. As I have learned from the ubiquitous food-related programs on Japanese TV, even the tiniest variations in regional cooking are of great significance and pride to the locals. I have had yakisoba many times, but the Shizuoka version is special and worth driving around for over an hour, according to my husband, because it is made with seafood.

Shizuoka is not an up-all-night kind of place. In an hour or so, restaurants will start closing, and then we'll have few options. Yoshi gives up on the navigation system and drives to a service station. He lowers the window.

"Where's the best place to get Fuji-style yakisoba?" he asks the cap-wearing attendant.

They have a brief conversation, and we set out again. He pulls into the nearly empty lot of a small privately-owned restaurant, and we get out of the car. Jio hauls the wheelchair out of the back and brings it around to Lilia's side of the car. The threshold is raised, but we get Lilia inside without too much trouble and settle at a table. We're so famished that the taste of the food, while tasty enough, hardly matters.

THE NEXT MORNING, we have breakfast in view of Mt. Fuji, and then we climb back into the car. We are at Disneyland as soon as the gates open. The aroma of caramel corn wafts out to meet us. Young women with Disney character capes and little girls in princess dresses flit about, while young couples in matching plush Disney character caps hold hands. What might be ridiculous outside the Magic Kingdom is totally acceptable here.

Ordinarily Lilia would be thrilled by the sight of people in costumes, such as the locally famous Sudachi-kun, a caped superhero with a green citrus fruit head. She is always quick to chase down mascots at the mall in her wheelchair, but here there are so many. She's unimpressed by the lesser-known characters. Snow White's dwarves and Donald Duck's nephews? *Yawn.* Nevertheless, they are all accessible. A lovely young American woman with flowing blonde hair and a pink satin dress approaches us. Lilia recognizes her as Aurora from *Sleeping Beauty*. They hug like long-lost friends.

The rides are less accessible. Although Yoshi and his students were welcome on Splash Mountain a year ago, the rules have changed. Now, if a visitor is not able to evacuate on her own two legs, she's not allowed on the ride. A little voice grumbles in my head. Why not make it accessible? Isn't this the age of universal use? I get that this is an earthquake-prone country and accidents happen, but at the moment, I'm not feeling the "magic" in the kingdom. I reluctantly take Lilia on a lesser kiddie ride. While we are airborne, she spots someone dressed up as Stitch, the extraterrestrial who lands in Hawaii. A long line quickly forms for a photo op.

"I want to shake his hand!" Lilia signs.

"We'd have to wait for over half an hour," I tell her. It's hardly worth it, and why wasn't she excited about all the other mascots she got to meet? I wonder, not for the first time, if she understands that there are ordinary people inside these costumes. She has always embraced the imaginary, still believing in Santa at the age of twelve. I never had the heart to tell her that the tooth fairy didn't exist. Lilia's world also includes ghosts and UFOs; she's enthusiastic about both.

"Next time," I say, knowing that Stitch's thirty minutes on site would be up before we even made it to the end of the line.

Lilia begins to sulk. Not even a handful of M&M's can cure her mood.

Later, near the castle, Lilia shrieks at the sight of another blonde American in a shiny blue ballgown: Cinderella. She speeds off in her wheelchair, her orange tasseled knit cap flying off her head. Ersatz Cinderella or not, I'm happy to see that her mood has improved.

Cinderella's Castle has a separate passageway for wheelchair users. A theme park employee ushers us onto the elevator, and Yoshi tries to make small talk.

"What was it like on the day of the earthquake?" he asks.

Is this guy really going to tell us? Wasn't this like asking a flight attendant about a previous plane crash while in the air? Wouldn't it be in violation of some Disney code to fracture the carefully constructed fantasy? Aren't we supposed to believe that nothing bad can ever happen at Disneyland?

"The castle really shook," the guy says. "It was terrifying."

I glare at them, consider cupping my hands over my ears and saying "lalalalala." This is way too much reality. And then, for a moment, I wonder how we would cope if an earthquake struck right then. Would we be able to get Lilia quickly and safely out of the castle? Is it even a good idea to have a roller coaster on a fault line? Maybe they are right to keep us off certain rides.

DURING OUR SECOND DAY in Tokyo, while we are making the rounds of Disney Sea, my son complains of a headache. I figure it's from the up-and-down rides, the sensory overload and too much sugar, but later, in the car on the way to the hotel, I discover that he has a fever. He sleeps in the reclined backseat all the way to our motel that evening

Our room is on the second level. There are stairs, but no elevator. I sigh. It figures. "Why didn't you ask for an accessible room?" I ask Yoshi. How could he have planned so carefully and forgotten this one very important detail?

He shrugs. "I can carry her."

Why make things harder than they have to be? Well, maybe next time he will remember. Then again, he has been brought up in a culture which values endurance, whether it be of enduring the pain of kneeling for two hours during tea ceremony or standing still in the hot sun for the ceremony to begin the summer baseball tournament. He is from a culture in which people abhor making a fuss. I, on the other hand, grew up hearing that the squeaky wheel gets the grease. If everyone kept silent, women wouldn't be able to vote, blacks and whites would still use separate drinking fountains, and there would be no wheelchair ramps in the United States, either. I think we need to be way squeakier in Japan. For now, I lug our bags up to the room while Lilia rides piggyback on her dad. Jio collapses onto the bed.

JIO'S FEVER marks the beginning of a month of sickness for our family. Just as he's getting better, Yoshi comes down with the flu next and misses his first week back at school. He goes into quarantine, speaking to us only by cellphone and taking his meals on trays left outside the sickroom. I wear a white surgical mask every time I go near him. It's the ICU all over again. However, in spite of our precautions, on the day that he's finally ready to go back to work, my daughter wakes up listless and warm. We take her temperature. She has a slight fever so we keep her home. This, the one year we have neglected to get flu shots, the bug is going around like mad.

I take my daughter to the doctor. She tests negative for the flu, which is a huge relief. According to school rules, if a kid comes down with the dreaded influenza, she's not allowed back in class for ten days to prevent infection. "*Kaze desu,*" the doctor says. A garden variety cold.

A couple days later, her fever goes down. "Now you can go back to school!" I tell her.

But she shakes her head, and points to her throat. She has a cough.

"Yes, yes. But you can wear a mask! It'll be fine!"

The next morning, she refuses to get out of bed. When she was smaller, I could force her out of pajamas and into clothes, and wrestle her into the car. By the time we got to our dreaded destination, she'd usually resigned herself to my will. But now she is bigger, heavier. I can't force her to do anything she doesn't want to do.

My husband and I both attempt to reason with her. She

remains firm. She's not going to school. The teacher calls.

"She's in 'sick mode,'" my husband says.

The teacher sends a message by fax. "We look forward to seeing you back at school. K-kun is worried about you. Here is the schedule for tomorrow."

The next morning, again, she refuses to go to school. I drag her out of bed, but she settles in front of the TV, still in pajamas. Exasperated, I lose my temper. "You're not going to stay home all day and watch TV!" I shout, shutting it off. My face contorts in anger and my fingers fly as I tell her that if she doesn't get an education, she'll be hungry and begging on the street once her parents are gone. This isn't necessarily true. Japan's social service system would take care of her, I'm sure. Even now she is entitled to a monthly stipend, to free health care and partial reimbursement of things that she needs, such as a wheelchair, leg braces, hearing aid, and cables for her cochlear implant's speech processor. But without someone to advocate on her behalf, she might very well end up in some sort of nursing home.

Lilia responds by grabbing a blanket, some manga, paper and pencils and locking herself in the bathroom. A little while later, she slides a note under the door: "Mama and Papa are idiots. I'm not going to watch TV and I'm not going to school anymore. I quit!"

My first reaction is pride. I'm impressed by her ability to express herself. She didn't begin reading until second grade, and she is far behind her deaf peers, not to mention her brother, who can read a novel in a day. But I'm also horrified at the prospect of my daughter turning into a shut-in, a "*hikkikomori*," or one of those kids who refuses to go to school or even leave the house: her entire social life dependent upon me.

I want her opportunities to extend beyond her bedroom, beyond our house, this town, this country, even. Until now she has been curious and motivated (she said that she wanted to go to Paris!), but suddenly she doesn't want to go anywhere.

This doesn't bode well for the future. I know that school is probably lonely for her at times since she usually studies one-on-one with her teachers. She has to pay attention and behave because she is constantly the focus of attention. Meanwhile, there are no classmates to commiserate with or pass notes to. It's probably not all that fun at times. But if she doesn't go to school, her options will be severely limited.

If she only knew how we fought against the pressure to transfer her to another school. If only she knew how hard others have fought in this country for the right for individuals with disabilities to have any kind of education at all. Although the first Japanese school for the deaf was established in Kyoto in 1878, and education was technically compulsory, children with disabilities weren't required to attend school. Furthermore, schools for the deaf were expensive, and few and far between. She has no idea how lucky she is to live only ten kilometers from a school where the teachers use sign language.

The teacher calls again. "You can't give in to her. The longer she stays away, the harder it will be for her to come back to school."

She's preaching to the choir. "I know, but what can I do? We've tried everything we can think of."

"Would you like me to drop by and talk to her?" she asks.

"Yes. Please."

Yoshi, who has often had to urge his own students to go to school, agrees that this is our best option.

Two of her teachers come over the following afternoon. We sit around the heated *kotatsu* table sipping tea. When Lilia sees that no one is angry, that she will be welcomed back to school, no questions asked, she gives in. Tomorrow she will be back in school, ready to distribute souvenir cookies from Disneyland to her classmates. I let out a sigh of relief.

Polka Dots, Forever, With Love

DURING THE REST OF THE SEMESTER, I help Lilia go up the stairs at the School for the Deaf to the third floor two mornings a week. She is in training for junior high school. She hangs on to the railing with one hand, and my hand with the other, raising each foot slowly and deliberately planting it down, step by step by step. By the time she gets to the top, she's exhausted and has to rest for a few minutes before making her descent. In sympathy, I sometimes walk up stairs without extending my legs all the way, as Lilia does. My thigh muscles quickly start to burn. It's tiring for me, as well.

We're both looking forward to spring vacation. In February, I learn of an upcoming exhibit in Osaka, two and half hours away by bus. The latest creations of the internationally renowned Japanese artist Yayoi Kusama—she of the polka dots, the pumpkins, *the polka-dotted pumpkins*—will be on display at the National Museum of Art in Osaka until the end of March. I've been intrigued by this artist for a while, and have a Yayoi Kusama-related writing project in mind, so this relatively nearby exhibit seems like the perfect opportunity to get to know her work better. At first, I'd been planning on going alone, maybe while the twins were at school, or while they were stashed at their aunt's house, but it occurs to me that

Lilia is old enough to enjoy and appreciate Kusama's art. Plus, if we go together, I won't have to worry about getting back in time to pick her up from school, or asking Yoshi or my sister-in-law to change their plans and look after her. Jio will be okay left alone. This would also be a baby step toward the mother-daughter trips to foreign countries that I dream we'll take in the future.

Of course, when I propose this outing, Lilia is eager to go. Art! A bus trip to Osaka! Polka dots! What's not to like?! So we make plans. But as she enters spring break and the exhibit draws to a close, I find myself dreading the trip. I doubt my daughter's capacity to keep herself entertained on the long bus ride to Osaka, and again on the trip home. If I go by myself, I can read, daydream, doze, but with Lilia along, I might have to chat, in sign language, for most of the trip. It will hardly be relaxing.

Also, I've been tired. A visit to my gynecologist last week indicated that I am a tad anemic; it's nothing serious, just a prelude to the Big Change, but simply going up the stairs in our house leaves me winded recently. Usually, going to a big city involves a lot of walking, and we'll be wandering around the museum. I'll probably have to push Lilia's wheelchair up inclines. I might even have to carry her. At the thought of physical exertion, I just want to cancel everything and stay home. But Lilia reminds me.

"We're going to look at paintings tomorrow!" she signs.

"Um, yeah," I say, casting about for some excuse.

On top of all my other concerns, we aren't really prepared. I was planning on showing her a documentary I'd bought about Kusama's life and work, and then discussing it with her. I've read the artist's autobiography, *Infinity Net*, so I know that she made macaroni sculptures because she was afraid of food, and phallic sculptures because she was afraid of sex. I know that due to mental illness, she has lived in a psychiatric hospital in Tokyo for the past thirty years or so, that she credits her art with keeping her alive. If she did not paint, she says, she would kill herself. In other words, I've done a bit of research about the artist and I have some context, but Lilia doesn't, not yet. Maybe we aren't ready for this.

Then again, it was I who wanted to see the Kusama exhibit in the first place. If I don't take advantage of this opportunity, I'll regret it later. And how can I allow myself to be defeated by a little fatigue? Friends and family older than I are running marathons, for Pete's sake. How will Lilia and I ever get to Paris if I can't even manage a day-trip by bus?

On top of that, my daughter hasn't been out of the house in three days. I remind myself that Kusama, who works with simple motifs, could be potentially inspiring to Lilia, an aspiring artist herself. Although some paintings and drawings make Lilia twist her cheek with her thumb and forefinger (the Japanese sign for "difficult") she could actually imitate the dots, the line drawings, the macaroni glued onto mannequins. Also, like my daughter, Kusama paints in spite of various challenges.

I want Lilia to understand the considerable hurdles the artist has had to overcome to become a world class artist. As a child, Kusama experienced hallucinations. She heard the voices of flowers and animals. She grew up in a wealthy, but dysfunctional family, and her mother forbade her from painting. She did it anyway. She even found a way to go to New York City where she made a name for herself.

LATELY I'VE HAD TO literally drag my daughter out of bed in the mornings. Although Lilia can't walk, or hear without her cochlear implant, she is physically capable of throwing back the covers, getting out of bed, going to the toilet, washing her face and changing her clothes *all by herself*. Even so, she has been lazy of late, making me wish for a winch and a crane. Now that it's spring break, I don't really blame her. But on the morning of our expedition, she is at her DIY best. She rises even before I do and composes a funky outfit: a black shirt with white polka dots layered over a white T-shirt with sparkles and a big pink heart, striped turtleneck, black and white striped tights, and blue and yellow striped socks. Perfect, I think, for a viewing of the art of Yayoi Kusama. She prepares her Hello Kitty rucksack and a handbag, making sure that she has her pink wallet, paper and pen, and books to read. She's ready to go before I am.

I didn't buy bus tickets in advance, as I'd originally intended, but I manage to get front row seats, the most accessible seats on the bus, both there and back. Thanks to the Japanese welfare system, Lilia's fare is half price. We will also be able to get into the museum for free: Lilia, as a person with disabilities, me as her companion.

We have a few minutes before the bus arrives, so we pop into a nearby convenience store to buy sandwiches for lunch and snacks to eat on the bus. We'll splurge on cake in the museum café later. I've already stuffed a bag of raisins to help with my anemia into my purse, but I buy some iron supplements and a prune Soy Joy bar containing extra iron for myself, and a chocolate CalorieMate bar for Lilia.

When the bus arrives, Lilia manages to hoist herself up the steps and into her seat with almost no assistance. I show the bus driver how to collapse the wheelchair, and he stows it in the belly of the bus.

There are not a lot of passengers now at mid-morning, and the traffic flows freely. It's a gorgeous day: sunny, albeit a bit chilly. Out the window we can see the lush verdure of the hills of Naruto. We pass the resort hotels along the beach, and then we're crossing the bridge that spans the Straits of Naruto where enormous whirlpools form when the tides change. I know that Lilia doesn't remember this, but a few years ago we took a glass-bottomed boat out into the midst of the whirlpools, and Lilia had been amazed at the sight of a multitude of jellyfish swarming underneath.

Now, she occupies herself with her book, her drawing. I read for a while; then feeling guilty, I propose a round of *shiritori*, a Japanese word game.

I let her go first. She writes "*momo*" (peach).

I have to follow with a word beginning with the final syllable. I scribble "*mokuteki*" (goal) underneath. She thinks for a moment, then writes "*kiiro*" (yellow). We take turns for another ten or so times before Lilia gets tired of the game. Next, I try to get her to review the English words I've taught her so far, but after a few minutes, she turns away, tired of studying. She just wants to be left alone. We cross over to Awaji Island, with its many onion fields, and then come upon the Akashi Bridge that connects to Honshu, the largest island in the archipelago. The glittering city of Kobe sprawls along the coast, easing into Osaka, our destination.

Once we reach Osaka station, we approach a cab. I worry that the driver will balk at the wheelchair, but he is kind. "Take your time" he urges, as I motion Lilia into the back seat. So far, so good. Within minutes, we're pulling up to the museum, and then we're in the lobby, preparing for a look at *The Eternity of Eternal Eternity*.

One might think that Kusama's oeuvre would be inappropriate for children. After all, at one time she was best known for her phallic sculptures, gay porn films, and for encouraging nudity in public settings as a form of protest against war. However, most of her paintings and sculptures are, in fact, child-friendly. The artist herself, who wears a bright red wig and polka dot dresses, retains an innocence in spite of her illness—or perhaps because of it. Much of her work is playful and whimsical. Also, children are more inclined than most adults to be attuned to an irrational fear of macaroni. In any case, my daughter is far from being the youngest visitor to the exhibit. Mothers and children in strollers fill the lobby and share the elevator with us as we descend into the underground museum.

The first gallery features a series rendered in black magic marker on white canvas entitled *Love Forever*. I hear a little boy say, "*Kowai!*" ("That's scary!"). I'm not sure if he's referring to the proliferation of centipede-like figures in *Morning Waves* or perhaps the repetition of eyes in *The Crowd*, but he gets it;

he feels Kusama's phobia, the intention that led to the work.

The next room is white with giant tulips dotted with large red circles—an experiential work entitled *With All My Love for the Tulips, I Pray Forever*. Lilia is delighted with the surreal space, the colors, the giant tulips, while I feel as if I'm in a Tim Burton film. We take several pictures, then move on to *My Eternal Soul*, in which many of the figures that appear in the black and white series re-appear in vivid pinks, oranges, yellows and blues. For a Westerner like me, these colors and images seem joyful and exuberant, but in Japan, where mothers hesitate to dress their children in bright clothes, and married women tend to don somber grays and navies, such hues are unsettling.

Lilia likes the colors. She pauses before the bright paintings, then reads the somewhat baffling titles. *Fluttering Flags*, which applies to red flag-like images, is fairly straightforward. However, the vibrant mood of a pink canvas covered with lushly-lashed eyes, a spoon, a purse, a shoe, and women's profiles contrasts with its somber title, *Death is Inevitable*.

Among my favorite paintings are the self-portraits toward the end of the exhibit. As a foreigner in Japan, I can relate to *In a Foreign Country of Blue-Eyed People* which recalls Kusama's years in New York in the 1960s, as a rare Japanese artist among Americans. Red dots cover the face, suggesting disease: dis-ease?

Lilia is partial to *Gleaming Lights of the Souls*, another experiential piece in which we are invited to enter a small room with mirror-covered walls. Within the walls, dots of light change colors, giving us the feeling of being among stars or planets in outer space.

Finally, we watch a short film documenting Kusama's life and work. There are no subtitles, but Lilia can see the artist at work, the assistant who eases her in and out of her chair, and who helps her to prepare her canvases.

"See?" I want to tell her. "We all need a hand from time to time." But I don't want to disturb her concentration, so I'm silent and still, letting her take in whatever she can by herself, and then we move on to the gift shop. I buy a catalog of the exhibit for us to look at later at our leisure before we head for the café for cake.

On the way home, I feel pleasantly exhausted, but hopeful. The trip was not as arduous as I'd anticipated. I'm also encouraged by Kusama herself, by the way she's found a way to make a living—and to stay alive—through art, in spite of everything. Later that evening, Lilia is eager to tell her father and brother about the polka-dotted tulips, and the chocolate cake. When she's explained enough, she signs "Paper, please." I give her a stack of white sheets, and she begins to draw.

IN APRIL the air is filled with swirling white petals. The cherry blossoms are in bloom. Lilia wears a school uniform for the first time: a navy blazer with shiny gold buttons, navy plaid pants, and a white blouse with a red ribbon. Although being a girly girl she'd wanted to wear a skirt, her teachers and I agreed that long pants would be best. Since she has to get up and down the stairs, she has enough to worry about without having to concern herself with modesty. Her seventh grade classroom is on the first floor, next to the woodshop. The room, recently used for storage, has been cleared out just for Lilia. There's enough space for a cordoned off dressing area in which she can change from her uniform to more comfortable gym clothes, and a sink for washing her hands and brushing her teeth.

Her homeroom teacher is Miss Endo, an intelligent and committed young woman with a master's degree in Deaf Education. She was Lilia's teacher in third grade, so they have already established a rapport. The rest of the seventh grade students, two boys, will be in their third floor classrooms for most of the day. Lilia will join them for lunch and for some classes. For this, she will have to climb the stairs.

In addition to receiving physical therapy at school, Lilia will go to Hinomine once a week with a driver I arranged through the Welfare Department at the town hall. Her new helper, Asami, has brassy dyed hair and a raspy smoker's voice. She doesn't know any sign language, but she's willing to drive Lilia. We decide to give her a try.

In addition to Lilia's teachers, therapists and drivers, I have hired a tutor to come to our house once a week. The tutor is a small, frail woman with a degree in Education, and JSL skills, which she picked up in order to proselytize as a Jehovah's Witness. She's also a talented artist, so sometimes I tell her to go ahead and skip the math homework and teach Lilia how to draw.

Jio has entered the junior high at his private school. He was offered free tuition because he attended the elementary school for six years, and because I am now teaching the advanced high school students English Writing a couple times a week. Although I'm ready to go back to work full time, preferably in a university setting, there are few jobs available. Therefore, I'll be patching together a variety of part-time jobs, none of which will earn enough for a mother-daughter trip to Paris. But I haven't given up. I've got some book projects in the works, some grant applications in the mail, and if all else fails, there's Kickstarter.

The Caves of Chattanooga

WITH SUMMER VACATION only a few months away, I make plans for Lilia and me to visit my family in the States. It's been two and a half years since our last visit. My parents offer to pitch in for a plane ticket. Jio is on the junior high school baseball team, and if he misses practice, he won't be able to play. Yoshi has to work. Unlike in the United States, teaching is a year-round occupation in Japan. During the summer teachers hold "extra lessons," patrol pachinko parlors and summer festivals to make sure students aren't smoking and drinking or otherwise up to no good, and deal with administrative duties. But there's nothing keeping Lilia and me from going to South Carolina for an extended stay. I have a bit of money in my savings account, enough for one more ticket.

At the end of July, we find ourselves in the Southeast on our first overseas mother-daughter trip. Of course, we're not entirely on our own. We're staying with my parents in South Carolina for part of the time, and we've made plans to travel to Tennessee with my extended family. There are others to help keep Lilia entertained and push her wheelchair.

I don't know what we are going to do in Chattanooga. I've left everything up to my sister-in-law who first suggested the trip as an alternative to a few days at the beach. Although I love the Carolina coast—the salt marshes, the frolicking dolphins, the sweetgrass-basket sellers on the side of the road—I concede that it's too hot to think about sitting by the ocean. I can imagine the white sand searing the soles of our feet, the sun burning our necks and shoulders. It has been one of the hottest summers on record, with the mercury topping the hundred-degree mark for days in a row. The mountains of Tennessee will be cooler. Plus, my fourteen-year-old nephew, an avid runner who's been on the varsity cross-country team since middle school, wants to run on a particular mountain trail in Chattanooga. Our destination is decided.

.

MY SISTER-IN-LAW is making the hotel reservations. I forget to remind her that we need a handicap-accessible room. My sister-in-law knows that Lilia can't walk and that she will need her wheelchair, but that doesn't necessarily mean that she will take this into account when choosing accommodations. Yoshi, Lilia's own father, rarely thinks to mention our special needs when making reservations. I recall how on our last trip, to Tokyo Disneyland, we had to carry her up the stairs to our second-floor motel room. Or maybe it's just that Yoshi, being Japanese, didn't want to impose, and believed that we could do everything ourselves.

I am often torn between wanting to do everything myself as a fiercely independent American, and wanting to ask for help, between being the squeaky wheel pointing out the injustices of the system and not wanting to make waves. I know that my conservative parents are often irritated by my insistence on political correctness.

One evening at dinner, just before our trip to Tennessee, my mother shares her outrage over new government regulations requiring every motel to have an accessible pool. My parents see this as an attack on small business owners. For me, it's common sense.

"By the way," I finally pipe up, hoping it's not too late. "We need an accessible hotel room." My mother looks surprised.

"Well, of course you do. Kavita asked for a handicapped room for you two."

I'm glad that this time, at least, other people are thinking about Lilia's needs, but I know from experience that consideration isn't something that can be taken for granted. Also, although I feel that others sometimes find my concerns tedious, I have to speak up. I have to do this for Lilia.

CHATTANOOGA, a town of brick and crepe myrtle backed by hazy mountains, is about a six-hour drive from Lexington, South Carolina, our starting point. It takes us a little longer to get there because we make a couple of pit stops; one is at a McDonald's where I find that the toilet paper and soap dispensers in the "accessible" bathroom are too high for a wheelchair user to reach.

With irritation, I pump pink soap into my own hands and wipe the goop on Lilia's. Does anyone ever bother to test facilities for accessibility, or is this all just for show? Lilia endures it all with nary a squeak.

Back in the car, Lilia occupies herself with a thick manga and a DVD with Japanese subtitles that we brought along as we cruise down Bobby Jones Highway past trees and trees and trees. About the only things of interest for many miles are the sign indicating the exit for the Laurel and Hardy Museum, and a couple of fawns lazing by the side of the road.

In early afternoon, we arrive at the hotel and convene with my brother and his family. Lilia manages to converse with her cousins through flashcards that she made in advance and Google translate (thank goodness for Wi-Fi!).

My brother has scouted out a cave from which we can watch bats emerge at dusk. We make plans to check it out the following evening.

NICKAJACK CAVE was once a refuge for Native Americans, and a hideout for pirates who preyed on travelers who came down the Tennessee River. Later, during the Civil War, it was mined for saltpeter, which is used to make gunpowder. At one time, the cave was even used as a dancehall, and it has been immortalized in song on more than one occasion. A suicidal Johnny Cash allegedly came up with the words for "Another Song to Sing" inside the cave. YouTube also turned up the tune "Nickajack Cave," by singer-songwriter Kevin Bilchuk, which is about how Cash found redemption while crawling around on his hands and knees in the cavern. In 1967, the cave was partially flooded after the construction of Nickajack Dam and is now a sanctuary and maternity roost for the endangered gray bat.

When I tell Lilia that we are going to view bats, she is scared at first. She knows bats only from horror movies and vampire stories in her favorite manga. All the same, she is willing to go. My concerns, as usual, are about accessibility.

We park at the Maple View Recreation Area, near the edge of the reservoir. Luckily, there is a boardwalk leading through trees to the bat-viewing platform. My brother and niece are already waiting when Lilia and I arrive with my parents. My sister-in-law and nephew have gone for a run around the reservoir. We can see their small shapes across the water.

It's about an hour till dusk, but already another group of three has staked out a spot on the platform: a young ponytailed woman sporting a pink T-shirt, shorts, and a nose-ring; another young woman with glasses, sitting on the railing; and a bearded guy with a long-lensed camera. The young woman with glasses is holding a net, and Lilia wonders in sign language if it's for catching bats.

The woman laughs when I inquire about the net. "No, it's for catching insects." Her sister, the woman with the nose ring, is a Ph.D. candidate at the University of Tennessee in the study of bats. She already has a master's degree from the University of Hawaii, where, she informs us, there is only one indigenous species: *lasiurus cinereus*, otherwise known as the hoary bat.

We can see that the cave is cordoned off, and a sign juts

from the water at the entrance, declaring it off-limits to human visitors. This, the bat scholar informs us, is to prevent the spread of white-nose syndrome, a disease that threatens the bat population. Once a colony is infected, the disease spreads quickly and has killed at least 95 percent of bats at some locations in only two years.

As dusk gathers, fireflies spark in the trees. Mosquitoes alight on my bare legs. I want the bats to come and eat the bugs. My sister-in-law and nephew return from their run. A family from Chicago joins us on the platform, and then a couple of guys and a dog in a boat pull up in front of the cave, the sound of the outboard motor disrupting our peaceful interlude. Their loud voices, twanged with Tennessee accents, blare across the water. "C'mon bats," one guy yells impatiently. Like us, they are here to see the gray bats emerge from the cave, but they are hardly respectful. They go beyond the sign, into the mouth of the cave, before anchoring just outside and diving into the water.

The Ph.D. student is horrified. She has explained earlier, about the special Tencel suits that students wear when entering bat caves, the extraordinary measures to which they go in order to prevent the spread of disease. "I hope they get rabies," she snarls.

One of the guys swims to shore and climbs up the embankment, then jumps ten feet from the cliff, splashing into the water below.

We wonder out loud if this is disturbing the bats.

Meanwhile, Lilia keeps asking me what people are talking about. She doesn't quite get this American custom of speaking to strangers. She thinks that we must all know each other. I try to keep her in the flow: now we're wondering if there is poison ivy in these woods; now we're talking about how those guys in the boat weren't supposed to go near the bats; now we're talking about how a scuba diver in pursuit of a giant catfish illegally entered and got lost in Nickajack Cave for seventeen hours twenty years ago, and how the cave had to be drained (the diver, David Gant, thought that his rescuers were angels and became a born-again Christian after the event, which became known as "The Bat Cave Miracle").

Finally, there is a speck overhead, and I point to the darkening sky. The bats have begun to swoop and flutter above the cave. First, just a few, then there are hundreds of them, a swirl of dark wings. They come diving for insects just above our heads, and then flap again into the treetops. Every night, between April and September, they feast upon thousands of beetles and moths and aquatic insects, devouring up to 274,000 pounds of bugs.

Lilia gazes in wonder at the bats, the fireflies, the stars in the night sky. When we go back to the car, the boardwalk is completely dark. We need a flashlight to find our way. It's too dark to sign in the car, but later, Lilia writes in her notebook: "Don't go in the cave! Bats! If you touch leaves, you will be itchy!" She also writes about the man who went into the cave twenty years ago and couldn't find his way back out.

THE FOLLOWING MORNING, we visit Rock City Gardens, one of Chattanooga's premier tourist attractions. There's a ramp at the entrance (so far, so good) but we quickly come upon steps. Our group has scattered by now and my wheelchair-bearer brother is nowhere in sight. I sigh. In Japan, I sometimes get tired of the hyper-attentiveness of the Japanese. It's true that strangers often rush to open doors, lift her wheelchair, and grab her arms while she tries to board a bus, but in an ideal barrier-free world, she would be able to get around by herself. And sometimes I don't want strangers touching my daughter. I just want us to be left alone. But now, I'm irritated by my family's lack of concern, and also by these damn steps. A Rock City employee tells us that to get to the Mother Goose Village, we'll need to go through a back entrance. Back entrances are for servants and delivery people! Why not make the able-bodied visitors go the long way? Why do we always have to make the extra effort? I try to shake off the gathering clouds. Lilia doesn't care. She's used to this, and her mood is unchanged.

There's a wide, sloped path going past various flowers and herbs. Lilia likes to take advantage of inclines and coast, whenever possible, but I hang on to the handles of her wheelchair. It's a good thing that I do, because I discover that the end of the path drops off into a crevice. She could have been injured, her ride twisted and mangled. Or worse. Okay, this is so-o-o not wheelchair-friendly.

In Japan, whenever I come across an obstacle, like a rural train platform without a ramp or a broken elevator, I sigh and think, "In America, this would never happen. There are laws to insure accessibility." But now I'm realizing that my glasses have been rose-tinted. My arms are starting to ache from pushing and pulling the wheelchair against gravity.

One path, "Fat Man's Squeeze," is too narrow for the wheelchair, so we have to turn around.

I decide to give up on the more inaccessible areas, and take Lilia to the Fairyland Cavern, a cave full of illuminated dioramas featuring scenes from Cinderella, Hansel and Gretel, and other well-known fairytales. I can't help thinking that it's a bit cheesy, but Lilia, who has been born and raised in the land of Hello Kitty, loves it without a trace of irony, and snaps photos of every display.

WE STOP BY A barbecue joint for lunch before hitting up our next cave on Raccoon Mountain, which according to the tourist brochure I picked up at a rest stop, is "rated number one in the South," with more formations than any other cavern in the region.

"Is it accessible?" I asked my brother earlier.

He told me that he'd called to inquire. "They said there are one hundred steps inside, but no more than ten at a time."

One hundred steps?

He assures me that he will help carry Lilia.

I'm feeling a bit dubious, but I figure that if Lilia can make it up three flights of stairs at school every day by hanging on to the railing, she can probably drag herself up these steps, too. So what if she slows down the guided tour? And if my brother wants to volunteer to carry her wheelchair, then fine. Maybe my able-bodied fourteen-year-old nephew will pitch in, as well.

We've already purchased our non-refundable tickets online via my brother's smart phone. We pass by a group of muddy-kneed spelunkers, just back from a guided wild cave tour, and go into the gift shop/reception area. The young guy at the cash register insists that we need a print-out of our reservation, and that the cave is not wheelchair accessible.

"But we called in advance..." my brother protests.

No matter. Whoever talked to my brother must not know the cave well. We can't take the wheelchair into the caverns. And our tickets are *non-refundable*.

My first impulse is to launch into a rant. *What do you mean this place is inaccessible? My daughter has a right to go into that cave and behold its natural wonders! You are discriminating against us! If Mammoth Cave can admit wheelchair users, then so can you! What about the Americans with Disabilities Act? And what do you mean our tickets are non-refundable?*

However, I don't want to ruin this family outing by making a scene, and we're already holding up the tour group, imposing on strangers. When the manager offers to allow us access to the first cavern and give us credit in the gift shop in exchange for our tickets, I'm willing to compromise. We have forced the staff to confront our situation. Maybe that's a start. Maybe they will consider ways to make the cave more accessible to wheelchair users in the future.

I would like for Lilia to be able to see the stalagmites and stalactites, the rimstone pools and flowstone, the so-named Crystal Palace and Hall of Dreams. I would like for her to feel the spray of the underground waterfall on her face and to be able to cross the natural rock bridges formed by centuries of mineral deposits deep inside. But when I imagine the additional construction that would be necessary to make this cave fully accessible—the concrete and drills and saws—I'm not so sure it's a good idea. Maybe not everyone should go into this wild place, especially if it would mean desecrating its natural beauty. Maybe like Nickajack Cave, we should let it be, a pure place of mystery. Maybe there are some places that Lilia in her wheelchair, and me with her, can do without visiting.

I urge my parents and my brother and his family to go ahead into the cave. Lilia and I wait for our guide, a lanky young man who takes us into the empty first cavern and shines a flashlight on rock striated like bacon, and a cave-dwelling salamander while giving us the official spiel. It's Lilia's first time in such a cave. She likes the sparkle of the quartz, the blue of the salamander. We learn that this dark place is home to a blind species of spider, and also to bats. She takes pictures of various rock formations: a straw, a stalagmite. Our guide lets Lilia hold the flashlight and explore as much as she likes, as long as we don't touch the cave walls. The oil from human skin can hinder the natural flow of water and mineral deposits. When my daughter is satisfied, we go back out into the gift shop, into the light.

Lilia goes straight for the stuffed animals on display and picks up a plush gray bat. I discover that, as in the case of Johnny Cash and David Gant, our evening at Nickajack Cave has made something of a convert of my daughter. Instead of being chiroptophobic, my daughter is now a bat fan. We get a T-shirt for her brother, and the stuffed gray bat to commemorate our trip.

WHEN WE ARE BACK in Japan, and Lilia begins to tell Yoshi and Jio about our trip, the caves are the first thing that she mentions. She tells how gray bats flew in a funnel up to the sky, how she saw seven states and scenes from fairytales, and how the stone in Raccoon Mountain Caverns sparkled. "*Kira kira*," she signs, her fingers wiggling in the air.

Okay, we had a good time. We saw some unusual sights and she found a way to communicate. I remember that when she was a baby, my only wish was for her to be happy, and she *is* happy. She's also lucky, I remind myself. None of her classmates have traveled as much as she has. Every experience, no matter how incomplete I may find it to be, will enrich her. Maybe I should try to be more like Lilia, who is often delighted by small pleasures: the flutter of cherry blossoms, the flicker of fireflies. I remind myself to try not to let my own disappointments dampen Lilia's joy.

Seeing "The Monet"

A COUPLE MONTHS LATER, I receive a letter telling me that I have been awarded a grant. In my proposal, I wrote of my plan to take my daughter to Paris and to write a book about traveling with a child with disabilities, a book about accessibility and adventure. After reading the letter, I burst into tears. This is a miracle! I now have the means to make Lilia's dream come true. We are going to France!

As soon as she comes home from school, I tell her the happy news. She launches at me—"*Yatta!*"—and we hug.

Yoshi is more reserved. "We need that money to renovate our house," he tells me. Yes, the paint is peeling under the eaves, and we need new tatami mats in the Japanese-style room, and new sliding paper doors, but this money is earmarked for Paris, for my book project. There is no way that he will change my mind.

"We're going during spring break," I announce. "Do you want to come with us?"

"I have to work," Yoshi says. And besides, he doesn't want to visit art museums and sit around in cafes eating macarons. Furthermore, France is not known for golf, his current passion. Oh yeah, and he thinks the French are snobs.

"I have baseball," Jio says.

C'est la vie. Lilia and I will go by ourselves, on the ultimate mother-daughter trip. We'll cruise the Seine, tour Notre Dame, and rise up the Eiffel Tower. But first, I need to provide some context. We have four months to prepare.

"Do you want to go see some paintings?" I ask Lilia. "With a robot guide?"

It's a Saturday, and we have nothing scheduled. Yoshi is playing golf, and Jio is at baseball practice. Left to her own devices, Lilia will spend the entire day texting friends on my smart phone. I've been thinking that she's old enough to enjoy the Otsuka Museum of Art in nearby Naruto, and that it might be good preparation for the Louvre. Plus, a quick look at the website reveals that since my last visit, a robot has started giving museum tours. Lilia likes robots, or at least she was a faithful and ardent viewer of the recent Japanese TV drama "My Girlfriend is a Robot."

"*Ikkitai*!" she says, pointing her finger in the direction of the door.

It's almost noon, but she's still in her pajamas and her hair is sticking out. She obviously hasn't brushed it yet.

"Hurry up. We'll go right after lunch."

She hastily changes her clothes and arranges one of her many handbags. She has a pile of them because they're packaged as premiums with the monthly girls' comics that she devours. This one features a fake fur flap.

I put on some makeup and change into a funky tunic and leggings, and a necklace made out of toys, in case we run into someone I know. One of my university students works in the basement café, after all; I don't want her to think that I'm frumpy. This is all very spur of the moment, and I have a nagging feeling that I should have prepared Lilia more. We should have made an earlier start, for one thing. We also should have watched some movies about artists, or at least reviewed the manga biographies of Van Gogh, Picasso, and Marie Laurencin. But if we don't get a move on, we'll miss the last robot tour of the day, and who knows when we'll have another chance to go.

I first visited the museum shortly after it opened, back in 1998. At the time, I thought it bordered on cheesy. Also, I was taken aback by the 3,000 yen entrance fee, which I defrayed by writing about my experience for an expat magazine. When my husband told me recently that it had been voted "Most Satisfying" by museum goers in Japan, I raised my eyebrows. After all, the museum doesn't house great paintings and sculptures. The works on display are ceramic-board *reproductions* of many of the world's most famous works of art. They're made of sand from the straits of Naruto. At the time, the grotto featuring replicas of ancient petrographs smelled of chemicals, not must, thus it was hard to pretend that I was looking at something old. The effect was undeniably fake.

WHEN WE ARRIVE in the museum lobby, the robot, a squat little guy who looks like a cousin to *Star War's* R2D2, is just beginning his tour. Although I'd read that Art can narrate in French or English, his default language is Japanese. Apparently, visitors have to make special arrangements to hear the tour in another tongue.

An elderly couple follows the slow-moving robot. Lilia wheels herself companionably at his side, even though I know she doesn't understand the words coming out. Ordinarily, she pieces together facial expressions, lip-reading, context, and signs with aural input to derive meaning. Art's lips don't move.

We accompany the robot into The Sistine Hall, where the *Creation of Adam* is replicated on the ceiling. Church music is piped in to create atmosphere. Now that the aroma of chemicals has faded, it's easier for me to pretend that I'm in Italy. Above us, a naked Adam and Eve try to hide their faces as they are driven from Eden. I wander to the front of the hall for a closer look at the Biblical figures in various postures, but Lilia is reluctant to stray from the robot.

Next, we take in El Greco's altarpiece with its gilt framing dark scenes from the life of Christ, and the Scrovegni Chapel, which is sometimes rented out for Western-style weddings.

The ceiling is a soothing blue, spattered with gold stars, but some of the images are disturbing. Lilia is impressed by the pictures of hell.

"Please enter the room of Pompeii at your leisure," Art the robot urges in Japanese as we move along. "I'm very slow. I can't go everywhere."

I convince Lilia to separate from our guide, to linger for as long or as briefly as she likes in the galleries. We step outside to take a look at Venus on the half-shell, her long hair coyly covering her private parts, flowers flying through the air (Botticelli's *Birth of Venus*), then move on to Antiquities.

The paintings were reproduced with existing imperfections, such as the divots in the 12th century fresco *Journey to Bethlehem*. There are no glass cases or velvet ropes to hold back visitors, no uniformed women sitting on chairs in the corners, ready to scold if a finger strays near a frame.

I skim over the titles of the works, but Lilia conscientiously reads the descriptions in Japanese. Since we are the only ones in the gallery, there is no current of visitors to carry us along. I like the privacy, but due to our leisurely pace, by the time we've reached the end of Antiquities, an hour has passed and Lilia is tired. "*Misugi*," she signs. *I've looked too much.*

"But we haven't seen the Monet!" I tell her. "Or the *Mona Lisa*!" There are still two floors to go, and less than two hours till closing time.

"And here, look at this!" I draw her attention to a reproduction of the medieval tapestry *The Lady and the Unicorn*. I figure it's a refreshing departure from the solemn Biblical scenes she's been studying up till now. And yes, she's delighted by the unicorn, the bright red background, the girl at the center of it all. She snaps some photos and we move to the next floor.

I try to interest her in Rembrandt's *Night Watch*, the bearded men with their frilly white collars and plumed hats, but she shakes her head. "Monet's not here," she signs.

Oh, dear. Does she now think that Monet is the only artist worth her time?

"Look at the lace!" I point out details in a Dutch portrait. "Look at those shoes!" I show her the interesting wooden clogs.

And then finally, we go outdoors onto a patio to view the reproduction of Monet's *Nymphaes*. There is a pond nearby featuring ceramic carp and water lilies. I try to imagine I'm in Giverny, but I can see the cars going by on the Japanese highway just beyond the museum. I can't help thinking how fake it all is. Lilia, on the other hand, seems satisfied. She insists on taking a picture of me. I take one of her, too, before the wall-length "painting." Mission accomplished.

With only about thirty minutes to spare, we rush over to view the rest of The Impressionists. I'm pleased to see a blonde woman in a red kimono: *La Japonaise*, also by Claude Monet. Lilia recognizes it from the cover of my latest book. We take more pictures. And then Lilia spots something that she recognizes from one of her manga biographies: a self-portrait of Vincent van Gogh. She pauses reverentially before it, reads the captions, and snaps a final photo.

By now, "Moon River" is streaming through the intercom system, indicating that closing time is drawing near. I regret that we didn't have time to try out the face recognition function of Art the Robot. I'm curious to know which painted figures we resemble. And I regret missing out on being served cake by my university student, and not having time to see *Guernica*, or *The Scream* or Gustav Klimt's *Kiss*.

Lilia is thirsty. Instead of the café, we stop by the vending machine selling Pocari Sweat and other Otsuka products. Lilia digs some coins out of her pink vinyl wallet and buys herself a chocolate CalorieMate bar. I doubt there would be such a vending machine in a museum of real paintings. I'm willing to bet Euros that you can't buy a Soy Joy bar or the like at the Louvre. In Japan, however, vending machines are ubiquitous. I ask a female employee to show us the way back to the special elevator that will take us to the garage.

"I wish we'd come earlier," I say. "There's so much to see, but it's expensive to come again and again. How about setting up an annual rate?"

"Well, admission is free the first Monday in June," she tells me.

Good to know, but I'm usually at work then, and Lilia is at school.

"Oh, and in August, after 5 PM, it's open for free."

Also very inconvenient. But what do I expect? This is a private museum, great for entertaining corporate clients, but not funded by the government and free to individuals with disabilities as are many museums. Still, it's a great place to learn about art and I plan to bring Lilia again sometime.

It's not until we get home that I realize I'd neglected to tell Lilia we were viewing fakes.

"We saw the Monet!" she tells her father.

Wait, wait. "That wasn't the real thing," I hastily tell her. If she thinks she's already seen all of the world's masterpieces, it'll be difficult to get her excited about the Louvre. "We'll see the real one in Paris!"

She nods enthusiastically. Then she mimes cutting off her arms and her head. She flutters her hands behind her like wings.

Ah, yes. *Winged Victory of Samothrace.* I laugh. "We'll see that, too."

Holiday in Osaka

I WANT OUR CHILDREN to be aware of possibilities, to be aware of the wider world, of cities and countries where they won't be considered strange due to their bicultural upbringing. In other words, I want them to grow up to be international. Yoshi, meanwhile, is keen on nurturing their pride as Japanese citizens. He was raised in an era when many Japanese were taught to be ashamed of their history—of losing the Pacific War, of the atrocities committed by Japanese soldiers in Asia, and of the supposed Japanese inferiority to the United States. Yoshi wants our children to know and love their country. Due to Jio's baseball schedule, winter vacation is the only time that we can travel together as a family. Due to our limited resources, we can't go too far. Yoshi proposes a short trip to Kobe and Osaka.

"How about a tour of the Glico Factory?" he asks.

As a kid growing up in Michigan, I remember visiting the factory where Beechnut gum and Lifesavers were made, and the Kellogg's Factory in Battle Creek. At the end of the tour, visitors got rolls of candy and packs of gum (Beechnut) or little boxes of cereal (Kellogg's). More recently, when Jio and Lilia were babies, we went on many a tour of the nearby *manju* (sweet bean jam bun) factory, and after viewing the various stages of sweets-making, sampled the confection of the day. Just say "factory tour," and I'm lost in a haze of nostalgia and longing for junk food.

"Yes!"

Yoshi signs us up for a look around Glicopia, at the headquarters of Glico, makers of Pocky (chocolate-tipped stick pretzels) and Pretz and our favorite brand of curry roux, among other things.

The gleaming white compound is located in an industrial park, which hardly sounds attractive, but as soon as we get out of the car, the sweet air entices. It smells like caramel, like candy. Hardly any cars are in the parking lot on this cold, sunny morning. It feels as if we are uncovering a location that no one else knows about, like we're Charlie about to go into the top secret world of Willy Wonka.

As soon as the doors open, we enter. A young woman guide with impeccable makeup and hair ushers us inside and invites us to look around the lobby. There's a display of the Glico company's inventions and accomplishments, along with photos of the many Japanese celebrities who have endorsed its products. We learn that the ever popular Pocky, which now can be found even in America, was born in 1966, around the same time as the fashion doll Ricca-chan, the First Man on the Moon, and miniskirts. Almond chocolate, another favorite of mine, originally came out in 1969.

Also in the lobby is a vending machine, dating to 1931, which might be mistaken for a six-foot yellow post box. The guide demonstrates its use by inserting a now obsolete one-sen coin into a slot. A small screen immediately shows the first thirty seconds of a black and white movie, and then a snack shoots out from below. To see the continuation of the movie, young customers could drop in another coin—and get another snack. Genius!

Before the start of the factory tour, we're invited to view a movie about chocolate. Luckily for Lilia, the movie is subtitled in Japanese. As there is no information available in English—

or any language other than Japanese—I'm assuming that few foreign visitors find their way to Glicopia. The factory is, however, ready to accommodate Lilia's wheelchair. We're escorted to an elevator while everyone else in our group takes the stairs to the fourth floor for the start of the tour. Although the guide doesn't use sign language, Lilia can pretty much understand what's going on by observing the action on the conveyor belts—the dough going into the cutter, the baked sticks coming out of the oven, the sticks going into packages, and a robot making cartons—and by reading the signs hanging over each station, which give simple explanations in Japanese.

OUR NEXT STOP is Osaka Castle, former abode to Hideyoshi Toyotomi, the guy who unified Japan. No longer a residence, the castle is now a museum housing artifacts from the "warring period." Lilia visited the castle a couple of years before as part of an elementary school excursion: a two-day whirlwind tour of Osaka, Kyoto and Nara. She's been inside, so we already know that it will be accessible. The rest of us have seen the elegant white building from the outside, but have never entered its rooms.

The castle is surrounded by a moat and a park featuring 1,250 plum trees and 4,500 cherry trees making it a prime spot for blossom-viewing in the spring. There is also an Osaka Castle Chrysanthemum Festival in the autumn; unfortunately, our visit doesn't happen to coincide with any blooms. Nevertheless, the sky is blue, the sun shines, and the castle with its black and gold trim is an impressive sight.

Although Yoshi inquires about accessible parking, we have to walk a ways. Once at the castle, however, we buy tickets from a vending machine and are shown to an elevator at the back, which is operated by a middle-aged woman. I've always assumed that riding up and down in an elevator all day, pushing buttons, is one of the dullest and least demanding jobs ever. In my experience, elevator operators tend to be as distant as the Beefeaters in bear hats guarding Buckingham Palace.

This one, however, assessing that we are an international family, addresses us in English at first, then switches to Japanese when she hears us speaking to each other in that language. I sign a few words to Lilia. Our elevator operator picks up on that, and signs to our daughter, to Lilia's great surprise and delight.

"I'm impressed that you know so many languages," Yoshi tells her.

"Visitors come from all over the world," she replies modestly. "I have to be prepared."

"Do you know Chinese, too?"

"Yes, and some Korean."

Jio, who's a big history buff, enjoys the exhibitions about the lives of the shoguns, the displays of armor and scrolls and swords. We venture onto the deck, wheelchair and all, for a closer look at the golden *shachi* (dolphin-shaped fish) decorating the roof, and a panorama of the city, the wooden temples alongside concrete and steel, the hybrid cars moving along the roads, the cherry trees and the telephone poles. At least two other wheelchair users happen to be touring the castle at the same time.

BEFORE LEAVING, we pose in costumes in front of the crouching golden tiger on the second floor. On the way out, Yoshi shows our new friend, the elevator operator, the photos we've taken of our daughter with a samurai helmet so big that it falls over her eyes. She brandishes a sword like a fierce girl-warrior.

"*Sugoi*," the woman says. And then she waves to Lilia. "*Sayonara*."

Some light is still left in the day, so Yoshi suggests a cruise by water taxi for a different perspective of the city. After a quick query, we discover that a landing point is nearby, so we hurry on foot and wheels. Unfortunately, the water taxi is not accessible by wheelchair; there are only steps, no ramp. But having come this far, we don't want to miss the boat (pun intended), so we board behind a Chinese tour group, my husband carrying our daughter to her seat. Over the loudspeaker, a taped voice narrates the sights between selections of American pop music, circa early 1980s. By the time we get off the boat an hour later, dusk has fallen.

"You and Lilia wait here while Jio and I get the car," Yoshi says, instructing us to wait on the sidewalk across from a train station. I hand her my cell phone to keep her busy, and she begins to compose a story about our day's adventures. Meanwhile, I see a woman in an electric wheelchair cross the street, zoom up the ramp leading to the station, and enter the building, presumably to board a train with equal ease.

JIO HAS BEEN craving okonomiyaki, a savory pancake that is a staple of family dining in Japan. We find a restaurant serving just that. It's busy enough to reassure us that the food will be good, but there are still a few tables available.

The server brings us menus in Japanese and English, and we debate our order in Japanese and sign language. When she returns to the table, the server, having noticed our mode of communication, signs to my daughter, "What would you like?"

I realize that things are much different in the big city. The area where we live is conservative and often backwards, but Osaka is clearly more progressive. Lilia might actually be able to live more independently if she moves to a more urban area in Japan. Although I would probably worry about her, Osaka isn't that far away from our home in Tokushima, and we could communicate by SNS and video chats.

"You can live here when you grow up," I tell Lilia, once we've given our order. "Everyone around here seems to know Japanese Sign Language."

She shakes her head doubtfully, not ready to imagine a life hours away from her family, but hope blooms within me. I'm thrilled to see that it's possible. She may feel differently in the future.

We have plans to visit Universal Studios Japan the next day, so Yoshi has made reservations at a swanky hotel about ten minutes away by car. While the kids and I wait in the lobby with its glittering chandeliers and plush carpeting, Yoshi parks the car and checks in. I amble over to the in-hotel bakery to peruse the bread. I appreciate that a ramp provides easy access here, too, and although the bakery is mostly empty late in the evening, I see that there is one other customer pushing a child in a wheelchair.

WE SPEND THE NEXT DAY at Universal Studios Japan, which happens to be one of the most disabled-friendly attractions in Japan. As the day winds down, the rest of us become tired from walking. It's cold. We're hungry.

"Just one more ride, okay?" Yoshi says.

We've been to just about every attraction but the roller coaster. Until now, we've all agreed that it's too scary, and I'm not sure Lilia would be allowed to ride anyway. Suddenly, however, Jio is full of courage. "Can we go?"

Yoshi shakes his head. He has a weak stomach, and therefore no desire to hurtle through the sky.

I look up at the cars rumbling overhead, listen to the screams, and square my shoulders. "I'll go with Jio," I tell my husband. "But you have to take Lilia to Hello Kitty Fashion Avenue."

"Deal."

The wait for the roller coaster is 90 minutes: the longest of the day, made longer by the fact that without Lilia, we actually have to stand in line. As we slowly inch our way forward, I note that I am the only middle-aged person around. Everyone else is at least twenty years younger. Maybe I'm too old? Will I need an ambulance afterwards? A video plays over and over, warning potential passengers to empty pockets, as a flying cell phone could cause grievous harm to those below, not to mention the phone would be ruined. A big sign warns us against riding the roller coaster if we are inclined to motion sickness (my husband), pregnant, have neck or back issues (well, my neck *is* a bit sore), or suffer from a lack of sleep (me!). Having waited this long, however, I decide to buck up and be brave. I hand over my glasses and climb aboard.

I can hear Jio screaming beside me as we lurch and plunge. My heart rate speeds up as we go around curves, and I'm hardly aware of the bright lights beyond, and the crowd milling about below. But the ride—the scariest of my lifetime—is over in a matter of minutes and we find our feet back on the ground.

"That was awesome," Jio says.

"Next time you can go with your friends. I'll stick to the merry-go-round."

When we meet up with Yoshi and Lilia, they show us the photo they've taken with Hello Kitty before a backdrop of pink, and the handwritten note, written by Ms. Kitty herself. In the photo, Yoshi grins and makes a heart with his hands. Meanwhile, I clutch at my upset stomach.

The Rose of Versailles

YOSHI MAY HAVE BEEN willing to pose for a photo with Lilia and Hello Kitty in order to avoid going on a stomach-churning roller coaster ride, but he wasn't about to drive two hours to see the Takarazuka Revue; especially not a production of "Oscar and Andre," a story adapted from the best-selling girls' manga *The Rose of Versailles*. Takarazuka, or at least the theater and its environs, has to be one of the girliest destinations in all of Japan. I'd been intrigued by the all-female theatrical troupe since I'd first heard about them twenty-five years ago, just after arriving in Japan, but I'd never gotten around to attending an actual performance. When Lilia jabbed her finger at a picture of Takarazuka performers in a travel brochure and said, "*Ikkitai!*" I knew it would be the perfect excursion for the two of us.

WHEN I MEET UP with my friend Claire for coffee, I talk about our plans to go see the Takarazuka Revue. Claire is about a decade younger than I, but we have a lot in common. For one thing, we are both originally from the cold part of North America. I was born and raised in Michigan, and Claire is Canadian. Both of us are long-term expatriates married to Tokushima natives. Both of us have an interest in the arts. Claire, who works as a translator and simultaneous interpreter, has given tours at the Otsuka Museum of Art. Last summer, she accompanied a Japanese theater troupe to the New York Fringe Festival, and before that, she starred in an independent Japanese film. She also has a daughter, and they're both eager to see the Takarazuka Revue.

"Why don't we go together?" I suggest. I've scouted out a bus tour, which would make the journey relatively painless. Claire went to Driving School in Japan and managed to pass the Japanese version of the driving test—both the 100-question written portion and the practical test *in Japanese*—but she hasn't gotten around to buying a car. I don't particularly want to drive. While I'm not a huge fan of group travel, there would be plenty of people around to help out with the wheelchair. I figure that it's also a way to introduce Lilia to the viability of group travel. She'll understand that in the future, if she wants to go on a trip, a guided tour (possibly with a personal assistant) is an option. She wouldn't have to wait for us, her family, to plan for her and take her where she wants to go, and yet she wouldn't be alone.

We take a look at our calendars. Claire's daughter has ballet lessons on Saturdays, Lilia sometimes has physical therapy, and I occasionally help out at my son's school, but we finally figure out a day that's convenient and book tickets to see "Oscar and Andre," one of Takarazuka Revue's signature musicals, now in revival.

In order to prepare, I borrow the two doorstop volumes of Riyoko Ikeda's *The Rose of Versailles* from the public library. I'd taken them out once before for Lilia, and though I'd seen her perusing the pages, I figured a review wouldn't hurt. Also, I want to read it myself. When I'd first heard of the series, I'd been intrigued. After all, it was set in France, a country close to my heart. I'd studied French from junior high school through college, and I'd been to France four times, including an extended stay in Avignon for foreign study my junior year. I'd always imagined that I'd end up in France, but then I'd been waylaid by love.

Speaking of which, love is at the heart of *The Rose of Versailles*, namely the impossible love between Oscar, an aristocratic girl brought up as a boy, and Andre, the poor stable hand taken in by her family. They grow up together, riding horses and fighting with swords, as boys do, and inevitably, their feelings change into something else. Oscar is called upon to be Marie Antoinette's personal guard. When she reluctantly goes off to Versailles, Andre follows, promising to watch over her.

After the first ten pages, I realize that I'll never get to the end of the story in time for the musical. I find the animated series on the internet, and watch the first few episodes, including one in which an androgynous bad guy dresses up as Marie Antoinette and takes her place in a kidnapping scheme. Lady Oscar, of course, spots the imposter, and manages to rescue the fourteen-year-old princess after a bout of sword-fighting.

I want Lilia to be prepared, so I urge her to take another look at the manga. She tells me that she's already read the whole story. I have my doubts, but I don't really know how well and how fast she is actually reading. At any rate, I don't want to nag her about something that's meant to be fun.

On the day of the musical, we meet up with Claire and her daughter in the parking lot at the bus station. We board with the other passengers, mostly women and girls, some who embarked in Kochi, three hours away. Lilia climbs into the bus without any help, proving that all that practice climbing the stairs at school has been worth it, and her wheelchair is stashed in the luggage compartment of the vehicle.

The girls sit in the front seat, while we moms take the seat behind them. They're equipped with notebooks for communication with each other, and electronic gadgets loaded with games for entertainment. I'm hoping that they'll get to know each other without adult intervention. At seven, Claire's daughter is six years younger than Lilia, but they can both write in Japanese. Even so, every time I peer over the seat, they seem to be in their own little worlds.

"She needs some time to get used to the idea of communicating with Lilia," Claire says.

I understand. Lilia is the first deaf person that Claire's daughter has ever met. It took me a while to get used to talking with deaf people, too. Instead of writing notes, Lilia draws a picture of Claire's daughter, with her long brown hair and button-up pink coat and passes it back to Claire.

As soon as the bus starts rolling, the tour guide's spiel begins. She introduces us to our "handsome" driver, asks us to inform her if we have trouble with our seatbelts or the temperature of the bus. She passes out stickers and tells us that if we go on lots of trips with the tour company, we can redeem the stickers for pressure cookers and pineapples.

As the bus cruises through the city of Naruto, along the inland sea scattered with deserted islands, fishing boats and tankers, our tour guide rattles off the names of some of the top performers, some of whom I gather we will be seeing today. She tells us about a junior high school student who'd been on a tour bus to Takarazuka such as this one, and who'd been inspired to pursue a career as a Takarakuza performer. Now she is a member of the company, and the star performer in her troupe.

"Perhaps someone on this bus will be inspired as well," she says.

We pass the Otsuka Museum of Art and begin to cross the Great Naruto Bridge. Off in the distance, we can see Shodoshima, an island noted for its olive grove. And on a clear day, the tour guide tells us, it's even possible to see Osaka Castle from the bridge. The bus makes a brief stop on Awaji Island. The guide suggests the onion cakes sold in the gift shop as a possible souvenir for the folks back home.

Aside from onions, Awaji Island is known as the epicenter of the earthquake that devastated Kobe eighteen years ago. The anniversary of the quake was only three days ago. According to our guide, the Japanese flag that flies at the rest area was lowered to half-mast on that day. The 6,000 people who perished are also commemorated by the 6,000 white lights illuminated on the bridge that crosses from Awaji Island to Kobe, on the island of Honshu.

As we cross the bridge, we are told that the color of the lights changes according to season and occasion. They are pink in the spring, when the cherry blossoms are in bloom, orange in fall, to correspond with the foliage, and green and red at Christmas time. Now, at mid-day, the lights are off.

We arrive at the theater two hours before show time. The guide distributes our tickets, and then we are free to wander. Claire, our daughters in their pink jackets, and I, head over to some boutiques nearby. There are hardly any men in our midst, and most of the shops are designed to appeal to the overwhelmingly female visitors. There's a pedestrian bridge painted lavishly with flowers, an eyelash salon, and a "fairy" jewelry shop. We come across a mouth of truth, copied from the movie *Roman Holiday*, and an ice cream shop.

We go across the street to a larger shopping center. The first thing we see is a large poster advertising Mr. Donut, featuring the transvestite essayist Matsuko Deluxe, who is a constant guest on the evening variety shows the rest of my family watches on TV. Somehow, a cross-dresser promoting sweets seems especially suited to Takarazuka.

We stumble upon a bookstore that has a full display of Takarazuka Revue-related publications, including a 'zine, which is now in its 84th edition and is published by the prestigious Waseda University. We head back to the theater.

As soon as the guide sees us standing in line, with Lilia in her wheelchair, she directs us to follow her. We get to go into the theater before anyone else, bypassing the hordes. "How lucky," someone says. "An escort!" I resist the urge to roll my eyes. Although I, too, sometimes feel glibly entitled when we're allowed to cut in line or get on planes before everyone else, I know that Lilia would trade her privileges in a heartbeat for the ability to walk. And I'd trade them all as well. We don't need the world's pity, but there's really nothing to envy about having to use a wheelchair.

We pass through the carpeted lobby, still empty, and take an elevator. Once inside the theater, we settle into our plush red seats.

The lights go down, the curtain goes up, and we are bombarded with pink and sparkles! Although the manga starts with the birth of Oscar, the production opens with singing and dancing. The principle performers each belt out a song, and there is a parade of women in ball gowns and "men" in white powdered wigs.

Lilia enjoys the fencing scenes, but later, during the long soliloquies, she doesn't understand what's going on. I was so focused on insuring that we had accessible seating that I did not ask about aid for hearing impaired audience members. Clearly, she hasn't read the entire story as she claimed. She looks to me for interpretation, but I don't understand it perfectly, either. The language is not colloquial Japanese. These are aristocrats, speaking *keigo*, an aristocratic form of Japanese. I look over at Claire, who, after all, makes a living as a simultaneous interpreter, but her chin is on her chest. She has fallen asleep!

"The women traded their husband's swords for money to buy bread," I sign to Lilia. "Lady Oscar didn't know they were so poor. Now she feels that she was wrong to protect the queen. She wants to help the ordinary people!"

I'm not sure how much Lilia knows already about the French Revolution. Since she doesn't have social studies or history or French, she hasn't learned anything about it at school. But maybe she's seen something on television. At any rate, she seems satisfied by my simple explanation.

"Her father wants her to get married now," I sign, "but she loves Andre."

Lilia understands this part. And she gets why Andre grips the banister in a later scene as he slowly descends a staircase. "He's blind!" she signs. So she must have skipped ahead and read that part. I'm impressed by her comprehension, and once again I suspect that her abilities are underestimated. At school, her teacher has her read simple picture books about animal friends in the forest, but she can obviously handle more complicated stories.

The love story is easy to follow, and Lilia gets swept up in the emotions of the final scenes. I see her wiping her eyes under her glasses as the story reaches its tragic conclusion. And then the star-crossed lovers climb into a horse-drawn chariot bound for heaven, which rises spectacularly into the air over the audience—a happy ending after all.

But that's not all! The play is followed by a series of songs and dances: a sexy rumba, a Lido-inspired cancan, and a Takarazuka version of that famous Marilyn Monroe-on-the-stairs-surrounded-by-men-in-tails-and-top-hats scene in *How to Marry a Millionaire*. This time, a performer in slicked back hair and a tux comes down the staircase while a bevy of women in full-skirted dresses bow down to "him." I notice that many routines showcase the *otokoyaku*: the actresses playing male parts. The biggest stars are the ones with stage names like Tom, Leon, Kazuya: the actresses who fill male roles. The implicit message in Takarazuka's musicals is that girls can do anything. As Lady Oscar shows, they can fight as well as, if not better than, men. They can be palace guards or samurai or Chinese opera singers! At one point in the story, Lady Oscar appears on the stage alone, considering her future. "Thank you, Father, for raising me as a boy," she says. "You have enabled me to have many experiences that I wouldn't have had otherwise." This line seems to sum up everything that the Revue is about: Opportunity. Empowerment.

On the way home, our tour guide wonders aloud if anyone on the bus was inspired by the story we've just seen. Perhaps, she muses, someone among us will go on to be a singer or a set designer or a dancer. It's a little too early to tell what effect this musical had on my daughter. On the bus, while doing her homework, she writes that she was "a little moved" by the story, but I'm sure there's more to it than that. For me, the fact that we managed a trip on our own to a new place (albeit via bus tour) gives me confidence to travel farther afield with my daughter.

The guide tells us that in the spring, the Takarazuka Revue will stage another story from *The Rose of Versailles*, this one centered on Marie Antoinette. I think we're going to have to miss that one. At the end of March, during spring vacation, I will take Lilia to the real Versailles.

The Paris Project

AS I START TO PREPARE for Lilia's and my upcoming trip to Paris, I remember my first visit when I was nineteen. Inspired by my brother who'd backpacked around Europe during his junior year of high school, sleeping on beaches and in ten-dollar-per-night hostels and on the decks of ships, I purposefully didn't make a hotel reservation. I thought it would be more fun to track down accommodations when I got there using my *Let's Go France!* book. Looking back from my forties, I can't quite fathom my teen-aged mind. *How could I have possibly thought that this was a good idea?* Maybe wisdom and hindsight make me feel this way, or maybe it's because I've been living in Japan for the past twenty-five years, among people who plan so much that they make Boy Scouts seem unprepared.

It was August when I first arrived, the month when everyone in France is on vacation. Sleep-deprived, jet-lagged, and dragging a huge suitcase, I found that most of the hotels and hostels were already booked. I sat down on a curb and resisted the urge to cry. At the time, I wrote, "Yesterday was hellish. After arriving at the airport, I spent the next four hours trying to get from place to place. In general, [the French] lived up to their reputation for rudeness. I was miserable—no one would talk to me."

Ultimately, I figured out the Metro, had a great time visiting the Louvre and sipping cups of silty coffee in sidewalk cafes and shopping at Fnac. A few months later, I wrote, *in French*, "In one month, I will be home. That makes me sad. I feel that I spent a very important part of my life here. I know that I will miss everything." It all worked out back then, but I know better than to show up in a foreign city with a wheelchair without preparation.

As a college student, I was perpetually broke. I stayed in hostels or the cheapest hotels I could find. In my journal I wrote, "The hostel is a dump. We have no sheets, no pillows, but it's cheap..." I wrote, "We're stuck in Paris and I have no money. Absolutely none." And, "I hate being poor in France." This time around, we at least have enough to stay in a nice hotel.

I search for "hotels in Paris" on the Internet and find around 2,000 places to stay. When I refine my search to "accessible," only about 200 come up. I choose a couple—a boutique hotel with a cat motif near the Moulin Rouge, and a former convent—and show pictures to Lilia. This is her trip, too, after all. She should be in on these decisions.

"Which hotel do you like best?" I ask her.

"This one," she says, indicating Le Chat Noir. "Because you can see the Eiffel Tower from the room."

Nevertheless, it's near Place Pigalle, where ladies of the night ply their trade—not really the best location for our headquarters. And although the convent-turned-bed-and-breakfast looks cozy, I'm a little suspicious of the narrow staircase. Is this place truly accessible, or is it like McDonald's, where there's a bar in the bathroom stall, but you can't close the door if you roll in with a wheelchair? Keeping Lilia's criteria in mind, I book an "accessible" apartment hotel near the Eiffel Tower.

"SO WHAT IS THE NUMBER one place you want to visit in Paris?" I ask Lilia, as we bathe together a couple of nights later.

She fingerspells, "E-i-f-f-e-l T-o-w-e-r."

No surprise there. Ever since we've decided to go to Paris, I've noticed Eiffel Towers everywhere. I'm not sure if it's a trend, or if they've always been around. At the local mall, every store seems to have some product—a case for chopsticks, earrings, a surgical mask, a welcome mat - featuring an Eiffel Tower motif. It is the universal symbol of Paris.

"How about number two?" I ask her.

"L-o-u-v-r-e."

And the third is the Arch of Triumph.

"What about you, Mama?" she asks.

Hmmm. When I was in college, I was mostly absorbed with learning the French language, with literature and movies and music. And with romance. I wrote in my journal about the Southern boy who'd broken my heart the summer before I left for France, and then about the Greek student I fell for in Avignon (and who was among the friends with whom I visited Paris on my second trip to the city). At nineteen, I equated the City of Lights with love more than anything else for which France is famous. Because of my limited resources, I couldn't dine on haute cuisine; I remember meals at Hamburger Quick, baguettes consumed on park benches. In the journal I kept while in France, I wrote more about F. Scott Fitzgerald than food (although there are many references to wine). But this time, I'm looking forward to shopping in the market and cooking French dishes with Lilia in our apart-hotel, and to choosing bread and pastries for breakfast, and also to our extravagant dinner at Le Jules Verne. And, as I tell Lilia now, "Chocolate!" I've been researching chocolatiers in Paris, and I am looking forward to seeking them out.

Lilia, my fellow chocoholic, nods and smiles.

"And I'm also looking forward to seeing Monet's paintings." Although I've been to the Louvre more than once, on previous visits, I didn't have a chance to visit Le Jeu de Paume, or Musee d'Orsay or l'Orangerie. There is still so much to see!

Back when I was a student, I visited museums and cafes

and Sacre Coeur, but, not wanting to be a typical tourist, I didn't even consider a cruise along the Seine, or an elevator ride up the Eiffel Tower, or dinner and a show at the Moulin Rouge. Lilia has no such concerns about the tourist/traveler dichotomy. She is completely unconcerned about what is cool. She won't care if someone figures out that she is *not actually French*. She's totally up for a ride on the bateau. And although she's keen to visit Mont St. Michel, which one of her teachers visited on his honeymoon, and which appears in every Japanese travel brochure, from what I can tell it's virtually impossible to navigate by wheelchair. I continue to explore our options.

I've never been to the catacombs, those boneyards beneath the streets of Paris. That might be cool, but also scary. Also, I can't find any indication that we could get her wheelchair down there. And although she's watched *The Bells of Notre Dame*, I know that she won't be able to mount the stairs to see the gargoyles up close. Note to self: pack a pair of binoculars.

"How about this hot air balloon ride?" I show her a website, thinking that it would be so Jules Verne to observe Paris from the sky.

"*Kowai*," she says. *Scary*.

As if to prove her point, the following day, news of a hot air balloon accident is broadcast on TV. Four Japanese tourists perish in Egypt when their balloon bursts into flames and falls into a sugar cane field near Luxor. The footage is aired over and over: a cloud of smoke in the improbable shape of a heart, and then a column of ash plunging to the earth. The bodies are instantly cremated.

In any case, I discover that the tethered hot air balloon at the Parc André Citroën will be under maintenance during our visit. And according to the FAQ on the website for the tour of Loire Valley castles via hot air balloons, passengers are not allowed to sit. They must stand for the entire journey and bend their knees for landing.

LILIA'S SUITCASE, the one I bought for her last birthday, is decorated with a hot air balloon motif. I'm hoping that it doesn't remind her of what she saw on TV. Now, as we count down the days to our departure, I think about what we should pack.

Paris is a fashionable city. According to one blogger, the better dressed you are, the better the service. I, for one, am looking forward to dressing up. For my daughter, this is a chance to eschew the navy polyester blazer, plaid pants, and white shirt with ribbon that she wears every day as her school uniform. She will be free to assemble her funky outfits and show them off on the Champs-Élysées.

A dinner reservation at Le Jules Verne on the second level of the Eiffel Tower has given me the perfect excuse to buy the gold-sequined dress I'd been eyeing in a catalog. Lilia and I go shopping at Youme Town ("Dream Town"), the nearby mall, to find something for her to wear to dinner. She's grown out of her formal clothes anyway. She needs something nice. We find a lovely deep-pink dress with tiered ruffles down the front at Zara. Shoes, however, are a problem.

Shoes have *always* been a problem. When clothing catalogs arrived in the mail, Lilia, at six, would get out a red pen and circle the things that she liked. Sometimes, she circled pink pants or T-shirts with winsome prints, but usually it was the footwear: black patent dress shoes with bows, red suede maryjanes, sandals with cut-out hearts.

The thing is, my daughter didn't need these kinds of shoes, nor could she wear them. Not then, not now. Because of her cerebral palsy, she flexes her foot when she should be relaxing it. She tends to curl her toes, so in order to get any kind of shoes on her feet, I have to slide my fingers underneath her soles and ease them in, making the cowgirl boots she covets pretty much impossible. Once on, they're always falling off. There is always someone running after us in shopping malls, down the sidewalk, in grocery stores, holding up one of the sneakers that has slipped off Lilia's foot.

Lilia is most secure in her $1,000-plus custom-made leg braces, which go all the way up to her knees. While wearing them, she can manage to go up and down stairs, and since, according to the Eiffel Tower website, she'll have to climb a stair or two to get onto the elevator, these would be most practical for dinner at Alain Ducasse's Michelin-starred, formal dress-required restaurant. However, the braces don't go with her purple dress. They are clunky and bright orange. I always let her pick the color. The orange is indeed pretty and bright; the color clashes with most of her clothes.

My friends suggest various options: a long skirt, leggings over the braces, some sort of futuristic leg shield (this from Ricardo, a Portuguese dancer, writer, and illustrator who is writing a fantasy novel).

Okay, so maybe I could sew up some sparkly leggings. And if we had a couple of months and a wad of cash to spare, we could have something custom made, but why isn't there something readily available?

"What's wrong with wearing the braces?" asks Susan, my Australian friend.

"Well, nothing, but I've noticed that on the weekends Lilia usually doesn't want to wear them in public. I think maybe she's self-conscious. And she has the right to be fashionable, don't you think?"

I do a search online and find that many others have the same problem. For example, in a forum for individuals with cerebral palsy: "I'm a 26-year-old woman who is struggling to find suitable (yet fashionable and attractive) footwear for everyday usage. I'm just wondering if there are any other CP adults like myself who also find footwear a problem? I would love to hear your experiences/suggestions on how you have tackled this problem or if there are any avenues I can explore?"

Sadly, there are no follow-up posts offering a solution.

ONE SATURDAY, Yoshi and Jio go on a road trip to see Japan's WBC baseball team play Australia. Lilia and I head for the mall to go shoe-shopping. She tries on a pair of black patent leather maryjanes, but can't get them to stay on her feet. At the appropriately named Monet shoe store, Lilia finds a pair of dark shoes decorated with leather blossoms. They're kind of expensive, but there is a strap that goes around the ankle, and a zipper in back.

The staff hovers behind us as I help her ease off her nylon boots and work her feet into the shoes. I know they're ready to jump in and help, but Lilia's feet don't work like other people's feet. Finally, she is ready to stand. They're a little big, and I'm not sure that her toes will stay tucked in, but she says they're comfortable. She says that they fit. I help her to stand, and she nods eagerly. I take a look at the price tag and frown. Still, they are cheaper than custom-made braces, and they will go well with the dress.

"We'll take these," I tell the clerk. We tote them home in a shoe box printed with an image of Claude Monet's *The Bridge at Argenteuil.*

For dinner, we have sandwiches made with French cheese, and *tarte tatin* for dessert. We're preparing our palates for France.

French Fever/Paris Syndrome

AS THE SCHOOL YEAR winds up, Jio becomes immersed in his studies. He has final exams, plus he's required to take an English proficiency test during spring break. Lilia, who is not on any sort of academic track, enjoys a variety of excursions: lunch at a hotel restaurant, bowling, an outing to see a professional baseball game.

There is also a week-long exhibition of arts and crafts by students of the School of the Deaf at a surf-themed café in Tokushima City. Lilia and her classmates have made things to sell at the makeshift bazaar: refrigerator magnets imprinted with matroyshka dolls, fabric-covered hair ornaments, cloth bags decorated with beads and flowers. Her teacher tells me that the students will use whatever money they make to go out for parfaits.

On the Friday before the exhibition closes, Lilia and her classmates go together to see their work on display. I go to the café to pick her up and to see for myself. The artwork is upstairs, in a loft. Lilia had to climb the narrow stairs, and someone else had to carry her wheelchair. She's still there when I show up. I browse the other students' paintings and prints, and then I find Lilia's work. She's spent nearly the whole year on a painting of a bird. But it's more than just a bird; there's a delicately shaded lotus blossom in the lower left corner, a shrimp, a butterfly. It's vibrant and happy and incredibly detailed. I'm deeply impressed and moved. I know how her entire body tenses as she concentrates on fine work, how exhausting this must have been for her. Yet she persevered over many months, patiently, laboring to get it just right.

A collage that she created in Art class of her image of Paris is also on display. According to Lilia's vision, happy people have picnics on the lawn in front of the Eiffel Tower while birds flutter nearby. Flowers are in bloom. There is plenty of cake.

Occasionally, I worry that Lilia will be disappointed. I think that I should warn her about pickpockets and Turkish toilets and the tiny, rickety elevators. I've heard about Paris Syndrome, a recognized Japanese malady in which young women are disappointed when Paris in reality doesn't match their preconceived ideal of the city. Supposedly, victims are subject to palpitations, hallucinations, and dizziness, among other symptoms. *That would be bad.*

Then again, Lilia is the sunnier, more optimistic of my twins, the one delighted by the simplest of pleasures. She exclaims rapturously over butterflies, heart-shaped pancakes and the first cherry blossoms of spring. How could she possibly be disappointed by Paris?

"Is it cold there?" she asks me.

"Yes," I tell her. "France is farther north than Japan."

I buy her a new coat, a nice one that she can wear in Paris with her deep pink dress and Monet shoes. I lend her a silk Chanel scarf to go with it.

I'VE DONE MY HOMEWORK and I know what to expect: Paris will be cold and gray; the ten-day forecast is full of clouds, with a chance of rain. I'll be pushing Lilia's wheelchair over bumpy, cobble-stoned streets; contacts in Paris and Trip Advisor reviews repeatedly mention that that the metro is inaccessible. The Paris College of Art, where I've signed up for a children's book writers and illustrators conference for the last two days of our stay, is in an old building that doesn't have an elevator; Lilia will have to climb stairs or stay on the first floor all day by herself.

Nevertheless, my excitement rises as we count down the days. When I tuck Lilia into bed at night, I kiss her, and sign, "Ten more days!" And then "Nine more days!" Till it's just "One more day! Tomorrow we're leaving for Paris!" By this time, Lilia seems a bit wary of my enthusiasm. All I get from her is a nod and a fake smile. Yoshi tells me that she has expressed some concern to him about flying and plane crashes, so her excitement is tempered with caution. I, on the other hand, am manic.

On the morning of our departure, Lilia dresses and stuffs her teddy bear into her backpack, which is already nearly bursting. I will find out later that she's packed six books, two of them hardcover. Plus, she wants to bring along a six-inch-thick girls' manga to read on the plane.

"Oof," my husband says, dragging our suitcases out to the car. "Why do you need so much stuff for only ten days?"

I shrug. I've packed two pairs of shoes and dress-up coats for both Lilia and me, in addition to our down jackets. We want to be fashionable in Paris. He's all about practicality. He wouldn't understand.

He cooks us a breakfast of spaghetti with spicy fish egg sauce and miso soup. Jio, too cool for demonstrations of affection, gives me a weak hug at the door, and promises to text the results of his report card, which he'll receive the following day, and then Yoshi drives us to the bus station.

ON THIS WEEKDAY, March morning, Kansai International Airport is blissfully empty. Normally, we travel during peak periods, but since spring break hasn't yet begun, there are few people flying out on this day. As soon as we approach the Air France counter, a young woman in uniform asks, "Kamata-sama?"

I nod, and she ushers us to the counter.

It seems almost wasteful to accept help getting through the non-existent lines, but I let us be led through immigration, through check-in and onto the plane, where I discover that Air France is one of few remaining carriers to have a selection of magazines available onboard. Air France also offers a wide variety of movies to choose from—nearly one hundred—in several different languages, but none of them are subtitled for the deaf in Japanese.

The flight from Osaka to Paris is twelve hours—plenty of time to watch movies, indulge in all-you-can-eat bread, play video games, and draw. On the plane, Lilia opens her notebook and begins what she tells me will be a manga story about a girl detective in Paris. We are situated near the accessible toilet and the French staff is far from rude. So far, so good.

After landing, we wait in the airplane at Charles de Gaulle Airport for the other passengers to clear out.

"You're a good drawer," the French flight attendant says to Lilia. I tell her about Lilia's dream to visit Paris. I'm proud that we haven't been any trouble on the plane.

Eventually, a couple of women show up with an aisle chair. "*Hoop-la!*" one of them says, as Lilia eases herself from her seat to the chair.

At the immigration checkpoint in Paris, there is a Japanese couple ahead of us: a young man, and a young woman in a manual wheelchair. The guy holds the woman's hand, pulling her alongside him. Lilia looks from the couple to me and smiles, delighted by this public demonstration of affection. And maybe she is also impressed to see that someone in a wheelchair, someone like her, has found love.

Bleary-eyed and exhausted, we follow the wheelchair attendant to the taxi stand. The driver manages to fit all our bags into his car. I help Lilia climb aboard—*hoop-la!*—and then we merge into the heavy late afternoon traffic.

As predicted, the sky is gray, overcast. I wonder what Lilia makes of the buildings along the highway which are spray-painted with graffiti, but I don't want to draw her attention to them. To me, after so many years in squeaky clean Japan, they look trashy: welcome to the *banlieue,* home of the disaffected youth of Paris. Then again, on my first visit to New York City, when I was just a few years older than Lilia, I'd thought that the graffiti was cool.

Lilia, apparently too tired to notice much of anything at all, is nodding off beside me. But then I nudge her—"Look! The Arc de Triomphe!"—and she perks up.

The streets are clogged with cars and pedestrians even though this is the off-season. Somehow I'd imagined the city would be quieter, calmer and that we'd be able to walk down the Champs-Élysées without bumping into anybody. The taxi crawls slowly toward our destination, past young men playing basketball in a cage a la New York City, past a Thai restaurant, and the Monoprix where I plan on shopping for meals. I'd imagined our hotel on a quiet side street, but as it turns out, it's directly across from a busy train station—La Motte Picquet—and there are people everywhere. A beggar with a cardboard sign sits just outside our hotel.

The lobby is a far cry from that of the luxury hotel we stayed at a couple months earlier in Osaka. Our room, down at the end of the narrow hallway, has a sofa bed, a desk and a stove, and a teeny tiny table, which is at the level of Lilia's knees when she sits in her wheelchair. Where would we eat our breakfast and dinner? And although I've requested an accessible room, there are no support bars around the toilet. There's no shower curtain and the bathtub plug doesn't work. I will have to help Lilia in the bathroom.

We do have a view of the top third of the Eiffel Tower, which juts above the train tracks like the pieces of an Erector set. Far from romantic, it looks cold and industrial under the gray sky. Lilia doesn't seem bothered in the least. She dumps her backpack on a chair and fishes out her iPod, preparing to take a photo.

What is this sinking feeling in my stomach? Am *I* succumbing to Paris Syndrome?

LILIA WAKES AT 3AM. While I loll in bed, she washes her face (something I have to nag her to do at home in Japan), dresses herself in mismatched print leggings and a cotton blouse, and applies tricolor nail art to her fingernails. She ties the blue Chanel scarf I've lent her around her neck, and fills out two pages of her Paris diary, which has been assigned by her deaf school teacher as homework.

"Couldn't you try to sleep until at least five?" I ask. Having downed a melatonin tablet, I'm still groggy.

She signs that she wants to work on her manga story. Who am I to stand in the way of creativity? I turn on the overhead lights and heat water for coffee.

We watch TV while we wait for the sun to rise: a cartoon about a girl named Zooey and her multicultural friends who said "*hoop-la*" a lot; the Finnish Moomin; and "La Famille Cro," which features French-speaking Cromagnons.

And then Lilia reads the hardback manga biography of Napoleon that she's brought along while I get dressed and arrange my indigo-dyed scarf.

Since I was too tired to hunt down a bakery the previous evening, we go to the hotel's breakfast room on the first floor. There's only one other customer in the room, a businessman, and the immigrant woman with a musical accent who keeps the bread basket full. She immediately clears a chair away to make room for Lilia's wheelchair.

We pig out on mini-croissants and little squares of *pain au chocolat* (four each!) to make up for the high cost of the breakfast. We fill our plates with ham and salami, yogurt and fruit, and try out two kinds of juice. Lilia has hot chocolate. I have more coffee.

"Do you want an egg?" I ask her, eyeing the basket of eggs on the sideboard.

"*Oui*," she says, trying out her French.

I bring one back to the table and give it to her.

She holds it for a second, then taps it tentatively against the table. It doesn't break.

"Do you want me to peel it for you?" I ask her.

She hands it over.

I crack it on the side of my plate, and the gooey egg white oozes onto my hand.

"*Ce n'est pas cuit?*" the businessman asks with amusement.

"No," I reply, embarrassed. "It's not cooked."

Lilia gives me a dubious look. Obviously, I don't know what I'm doing in this country.

FUELED BY massive amounts of carbohydrates, we are now ready to take on the Louvre. We head for the taxi stand across the street where a cab lingers. The young driver doesn't seem particularly motivated at first, but after establishing that the wheelchair is indeed collapsible—"*Oui, c'est pliable!*" I say, smashing my hands together—he deigns to give us a ride.

Unaccustomed to taxis, Lilia and I are a bit intimidated about riding in a stranger's car in a foreign country. All three of us are silent. The only sound is that of a shutter clicking as Lilia snaps photos of a corner chocolate shop next to a Starbucks, steps descending into the metro, a small white car with a bicycle strapped to the back of it, and a stone column topped by a gilded griffin. But when we veer past the Eiffel Tower, I can't help myself. "Look!" I nudge Lilia.

"Waaa!"

And then I see a building on the right with a golden dome. "*Qu'est-ce c'est*?" I ask.

"*Les Invalides*," the driver replies, thawing.

"That's where Napoleon is buried," I tell Lilia excitedly.

The rest of the way, our driver helpfully points out sights: Le Grand Palais, with its window-covered roof; the Pont d'Alexandre, a bridge as ornate as a wedding cake; La Place de la Concorde and finally, le Louvre. A dark-haired woman in an ultramodern orange jacket and black leggings race-walks past the majestic, sprawling stone museum.

It's still early. We line up outside I.M. Pei's futuristic Pyramid along with a tour group from Japan.

"They're Japanese," I sign to Lilia.

"I know," she signs back, patting her chest with a touch of impatience. "There are lots of Japanese in Paris." Apparently, her teacher, the one who'd come to Paris on his honeymoon, has already told her all about that.

There are signs warning about pickpockets, but surrounded by Japanese tourists, I feel safe. I notice there are several other mothers and daughters there together.

When the museum finally opens, we are escorted to an open-air elevator which takes us from the hothouse interior of the pyramid down to the first floor of the Louvre.

The museums of Paris are free to students, the unemployed, and those with disabilities along with a companion. I love the idea that art is for everyone, and that no one should be denied due to financial or physical circumstances. Also, I'm glad that we don't have to wait in line.

A woman at the information desk gives me a map indicating routes for wheelchair users.

"If you want to start with the *Mona Lisa*, take that elevator," she says.

I thank her, and without consulting the map, we start to explore.

One of the first things that any visitor to the Louvre sees is *Winged Victory of Samothrace*.

Lilia immediately identifies the headless, armless, winged woman sculpture. "*Pari no Koibito!*" she signs. *Paris Lovers!*

The previous weekend, we watched the movie *Funny Girl* (*Pari no Koibito*, in Japanese) in which Audrey Hepburn stars as an ugly duckling model. In one of the most famous scenes, during a photo shoot with Fred Astaire, she descends the stairs in front of *Winged Victory of Samothrace* saying, "Take the picture! Take the picture!" On this day, a lot of people are taking pictures. I run up to the top of the steps and take a few of the sculpture myself, then snap one of Lilia, waiting patiently at the bottom.

We move on. Next, we find ourselves in a gallery full of

statues: a well-preserved horse's head, headless sphinxes, and the ripped torsos of pre-classic Greece. Two black women in smocks dust a marble lion, using rainbow-colored feather dusters.

There's hardly anyone else in the room, and I think of my friend Claire who'd come to Paris on her honeymoon. She told me that when she and her new husband visited the Louvre, they'd first gone to see the least popular African and Asian exhibits because they felt sorry for the lack of visitors. But then they'd regretted not having enough time to see the more famous works of art. Supposedly, it would take weeks to see everything in the museum, especially if you are carefully observing each painting or sculpture or pottery shard.

Lilia pauses at each glass case, taking pictures of what most interests her, which seems to be everything. Finally, she whips out her sketchbook and pencil case and begins to draw a headless statue. I'm not wearing a watch, but I figure we've spent close to twenty minutes in this one gallery that doesn't even house anything famous.

At our last parent-teacher conference of the school year, Lilia's teacher, Miss Endo, and I discussed the importance of time management. Lilia had spent nearly the entire scholastic year working on her bird painting, shading the leaves of a lotus flower just so, adding a butterfly here, a blade of grass there. The painting turned out beautifully, and I had admired her patience, her persistence, and her attention to detail. Miss Endo, however, thought that Lilia needed to learn how to meet deadlines. In the eighth grade, she suggested, Lilia would have to finish her projects within a certain amount of time. This made me feel sad, and a little angry at the time, but now, waiting for Lilia to finish her sketch, I find myself in accord with her teacher. There is so much to see in this vast warren of galleries, but at this rate, she will once again be tired of looking before we even get out of the antiquities.

I wait till she's finished her sketch, complete with label, date, and signature. Then I wheel her into the adjoining exhibit of Islamic Art, where French schoolchildren of all skin colors are laying on the floor with their own sketchbooks, while teachers scurry around, reminding them to be quiet.

"Let's go find the *Mona Lisa*," I suggest.

The galleries full of paintings are more popular. It's easy to tell which paintings are most famous, because they've drawn the largest crowds. At least two guided tour groups are assembled in front of *The Coronation of Napoleon*, a huge painting that takes up nearly an entire wall. Lilia recognizes the painting, or at least Napoleon, and begins snapping pictures. She photographs Napoleon on his horse, and Napoleon in the midst of battle, and also Joan of Arc, the subject of another manga biography she read before embarking on this trip.

In the next gallery, the crowd around the *Mona Lisa* is impenetrable. It's the only painting that has been cordoned off, and the only one that every visitor absolutely has to see. While I'm standing there trying to figure out how to forge a path, a tall Chinese guy taps on some shoulders and calls out, and within seconds, the way is cleared for Lilia. I hang back while she wheels herself forward. Between the bodies, I glimpse the docent guarding the painting release the velvet rope and invite Lilia—*only Lilia* - inside the cordoned-off area. She takes a photo and then rolls back to me with a huge smile.

"I saw the real *Mona Lisa*!" she signs. "I took a picture!"

"I know! Isn't that great?"

I don't bother to fight through the crowd. I've seen the *Mona Lisa* before, after all. My attention is drawn instead to another 16th century Italian painting in the Carre gallery, *Esther and Assuerus*, which was collected by Louis XI. This painting depicts Esther, the favorite wife of the Persian King Xerxes (who sits on a throne), as she faints upon hearing the news that the decree ordering the destruction of her people, the Jews, has been lifted. What strikes me, however, is not the lovingly detailed garments of Queen Esther, nor the dog curled up in the corner, but the little person who appears to be part of the king's court. His skin is black, his chin is bearded, and his hand is on his sword. He is clearly an adult, but he can't be any more than three feet tall. He has what we would today consider special needs, but he fits seamlessly into this tableau. I point him out to Lilia, who takes a picture, of course. I continue thinking about the figure as we go in search of the *Venus de Milo*.

Attempting to follow the map, I get us as far as the staircase leading up to the famed statue. It's only a few steps, so I make as if to help Lilia climb them. A woman rushes up to us, "*Non!*" she says. "You must take the elevator!"

And so we go back in search of elevator B or C, or whichever one we were supposed to take. There are so many elevators in this rabbit-warren of a palace, and each one goes to a very specific destination. I keep running into the same humorless guard.

"Isn't this the way to the *Venus de Milo*?" I ask.

"Yes, but there are stairs. You must go back."

And around and around we go.

Even more difficult than finding that particular statue, however, is locating a wheelchair-accessible bathroom. In spite of having downed two glasses of juice and a cup of hot chocolate, my daughter is like a camel. She can hold it forever. I, however, have a fortysomething bladder, and I've drunk three cups of coffee. I ask a young woman for directions. I never would have found the bathroom myself. There's no neon sign, no stick woman in a skirt. The door is disguised as a regular wall, and there is only one toilet. We take care of our business and locate the woman sans arms that we've been searching for, and then look at some other paintings and sculptures of fleshy, indolent women and perfectly toned men, and then we decide it's time for lunch.

We make our way towards the entrance, tagging along behind a group of visitors in wheelchairs and their attendants. They are all listening to guided tours on audio. I realize that if we'd asked for a guide, we would have avoided wandering around aimlessly, looking for elevators, but it's too late for that. In any case, Lilia has already taken close to a hundred photos. We've seen quite a bit.

We eat in a cafeteria off the lobby, amidst other tourists speaking half a dozen different languages. The ceiling is striped with red. While I finish my curry chicken wrap, Lilia pores over the Japanese version of the *Pocket Guide to the Louvre*.

I'm not sure how much she understands. At our last parent-teacher conference, the week before, Miss Endo told me that, according to tests, Lilia reads at a second grade level.

"The end of the second grade," she'd clarified.

Still, she was way behind her peers.

I felt discouraged. I'd seen her reading young adult books, books without illustrations, pages of words! In fact, three of the books she'd brought along - a novel and two short story collections - were intended for young adults. But maybe she was just skimming, skipping over unfamiliar kanji and chunks of text that she didn't understand, much in the way that I read Japanese.

I knew that I was partly to blame for Lilia's low reading ability. Many of her deaf school peers, spurred on by "education mamas," were reading and writing at the age of three. I, on the other hand, had struggled to memorize the forty-four signs corresponding to the Japanese phonetic alphabet. And although I'd tried to sign the stories of picture books to Lilia, she was usually eager to turn the page before I'd gotten through the words. If only I had been better able to communicate with my daughter in Japanese! Because I was raising her in a second language, she was at a disadvantage, but at least I knew Japanese Sign Language better than anyone else in our family.

Her health was another factor. She'd spent a year and a half in and out of the hospital for various respiratory illnesses. Every trip to the ICU was a set-back. While other kids her age had been learning numbers and colors and names of animals, she'd been struggling to simply stay alive.

Lilia didn't begin to read fluently until she was in third or fourth grade. To me it was something of a miracle that she was reading at all. And I know that even though she isn't anywhere near grade level, she's extracting information from books. She knows, for example, that desperate people jump from the Eiffel Tower in order to commit suicide. She also knows that the *Mona Lisa* has once been stolen from the Louvre by a person who worked in the museum—a janitor, she said. I hadn't known these things, and I'm delighted to learn them from Lilia. I also know that she is capable of absorbing and understanding information and that her knowledge of Japanese, of history, of the world, will continue to grow.

AFTER WE FINISH our lunch, we return to the open-air elevator that ascends to I.M. Pei's Pyramid since that seems to be the only way out. The entrance is cordoned off by stretchy tape, and two museum workers lean against it. When we approach, one of them, a woman of Asian extraction, languidly moves to activate the elevator.

I encourage Lilia to take a photo of it, since she's taken pictures of just about everything else in the Louvre. Meanwhile, I wait for the woman to lift the barrier. She says something to me in French that I don't quite catch. I'm tired, remember. Jet-lagged. And it has been at least fourteen years since I've used my college French. Maybe she said "*Prends-le.*" *Take it.* I'm not sure. In any case, I figure out that she's waiting for us to get on the elevator. I make as if to duck under the tape, and she rolls her eyes. "*Ai-yai-yai!*" she says, as if she cannot believe my stupidity. She gazes off into the distance. *French people are rude,* I remind myself.

I unlatch the tape myself, and we get the heck out of there.

WE WALK ALONG the Jardins des Tuileries, taking photos of the white statues positioned at intervals. Off to the sides, bare tree branches scratch at the blue sky. A group of blind people tap white canes along the gravel path. An Asian woman in a leopard-print coat and sunglasses sits in a green metal chair at one of two ponds, basking in the late afternoon sun. African immigrants try to sell us Eiffel Tower keychains for one euro each. I buy two, but the seller seems irritated with me. *Why won't I buy more?*

We finally make it to the end of the esplanade, to L'Orangerie, with its double columns on both sides of the front entrance, a museum I've never visited before.

"Let's go see the real Monet," I say, trying to pump up Lilia. I'm worried that she's had enough of art for one day, but she doesn't protest.

We find the accessible entrance and are waved through. I push Lilia into a white circular room. Many visitors sit on a bench at the center, taking in the blues and greens of the light-dappled pond at Giverny. A young woman with multiple piercings sits on the carpeted floor, talking on her cellphone.

Lilia wants to sketch. I hand over her sketchbook and pencil case, and she begins to draw her version of the lily pads.

A guy with a pierced eyebrow comes into the gallery and sits down on the carpet.

WHEN I VISITED Paris in my twenties, I'd gotten around by the metro. It was cheap, fast, and oh-so Parisian. Having mastered the various lines, I'd felt like Queen of the Tracks. But it was underground, so I never got a clear idea of distances, and where the various landmarks were in relation to one another.

Now I see that there are many ways to get around Paris above ground, including Velib, the bicycle rental system, pedicabs (which don't seem to have storage space for a wheelchair), and Segways (which require users to stand). For our purposes, a taxi seems to be the best bet.

After we exit l'Orangerie and buy a few postcards near the Place de la Concorde, I decide to look around for a cab. I push Lilia's wheelchair through a bunch of red and white Thai-style tuk-tuks, which are sort of like noisy golf carts. Their drivers are loitering about, waiting for passengers.

"Where are you going?" one asks me.

I tell him that we're staying across from La Motte Picquet station, near the Eiffel Tower. I hadn't considered a tuk-tuk, thinking that there was no room for Lilia's wheelchair, but the man doesn't seem put off.

"I'll take you there for thirty euros," he tells me.

That's ten euros more than it cost to get us to the Louvre this morning. I politely refuse, telling him it's too expensive for me. I'm trying to stick to a 100 euro per diem. Even with free admission to the museums, after the morning's taxi ride, lunch, and that copy of the *Pocket Guide to the Louvre*, we've barely got enough money left for groceries for dinner.

Another driver, a slightly younger guy, approaches. "I'll take you for fifteen," he says.

It sounds like a good deal. "Okay!"

And so we climb into the tuk-tuk, which, to my surprise, has a navigation system, and then we're in the midst of crazy Parisian traffic. There are no lines dividing the avenues into the teeming lanes. It seems wild and dangerous. The wind whips our hair, and the loud *tuk tuk tuk* of the engine fills our ears.

Lilia is all smiles. "*Tanoshii!*" she says. Fun!

She takes pictures, while I wonder how much I'm supposed to tip this guy. I have a memory of a disgruntled taxi driver in Avignon, throwing coins into the street when my friend and I apparently tipped too little.

We finally pull up in front of the hotel. While the driver gets Lilia's wheelchair out of the back, I dig into my purse.

He waves off my money. "Free!" he says.

It feels a bit like charity, but I decide to chalk it up to Lilia's charm. Why not? We'll put the unexpected euros toward dinner.

The driver poses as Lilia takes his picture.

"*Merci!*" we shout after him.

Back in our apartment hotel, I prepare a simple dinner of ham, salad, and bread from the Monoprix next door. Although the table is too small and low for the wheelchair, the desk is just the right height. I spread a cloth napkin over the desk and Lilia and I have our dinner there, side by side. If we look to the right, we can see the top of the Eiffel Tower. Perfect.

"Is Paris the way you imagined it would be?" I ask her as we finish off our meal with a raspberry tart.

She replies without hesitation: "Yes."

Later, I sit by the window, sipping a glass of "bio" wine while Lilia sends texts. When dusk falls, the Eiffel Tower lights up like a beacon. At eight o'clock, it begins to sparkle, as if there is a birthday or a celebration.

"Look, Lilia!"

Later, I will realize that it sparkles every hour for five minutes, every night. As we watch those dancing lights, it's easy to imagine that the show is just for us, Lilia and me, finally together here in Paris. I find myself falling in love with the city all over again.

War and Peace and Napoleon

I'VE ALWAYS HAD A THING for Napoleon Bonaparte. After all, he was a pretty amazing guy. In addition to his military exploits, he oversaw the centralization of the French government, established the Bank of France, got the French people to accept the metric system, reformed the law (the Napoleonic Code still forms the basis of legal process in a quarter of the world), and instituted a tax code, and road and sewer systems. He was passionate about his wife Josephine, even if he had to divorce her in order to produce an heir, and he was also pretty cute, if the paintings hanging on the walls of the Louvre are anything to go by. He was not perfect, of course. Bonaparte re-established slavery in the French colonies, had mistresses, and was responsible for the deaths of many men, but he has played an undeniable role in the formation of France.

Since our hotel is near the military academy where Napoleon was educated and Les Invalides where he is now entombed, I think it would be a waste not to visit these sites. I wasn't sure, however, if Lilia would be interested or if she even had any idea of who he was.

"Have you ever heard of Napoleon?" I'd asked her back in Japan.

"Yes!" she said. She'd read about him, or maybe seen something about him on TV.

Oh, good. I'd raided my son's bookcase and come up with another book—a book about French history in manga, which I encouraged her to review. She'd brought it along in her suitcase.

On our second morning in Paris, Lilia writes a postcard to her former homeroom teacher, Miss Endo, and then we set off for a morning devoted to Napoleon.

I ascertained from our taxi ride the day before that Les Invalides is within walking distance. I want to walk as much as possible to make up for the buttery almond croissant I've eaten, and also to save money.

We walk past the military academy, past a homeless man camped out on the corner, past a *mademoiselle* with pink hair, till we finally come to the entrance of the Military Museum. Verdigris canons are aimed at the road. Impeccably trimmed shrubs are lined up in front. The tricolor flag waves from the crown of the building.

We've gotten there early and we don't have to wait in line for tickets, so we are the first ones inside. A close-cropped guard lets us in through a special entrance.

We take a look at dolls dressed in military attire through the ages.

"How could you ride a horse in that?" I wonder aloud to Lilia, while pointing to a tin-man costume with a slit for the eyes. There are other figures dressed in chain mail, or in helmets adorned with lavish plumes, or in tunics with baggy red trousers. Lilia lingers before each of the glass cases. I hurry her along. There is so little time! And so much to see!

The guard directs us onto the elevator. We get off at the first floor where there is an extensive exhibit devoted to World War II, including a video showing Japanese kamikaze pilots downing ceremonial cups of sake before they fly off to their destruction.

Lilia is familiar with WWII. As a family, we visited the Peace Museum in Hiroshima where she'd seen photos of victims of the atomic bomb dropped by Americans. Lilia had later done a school presentation on the bombing, and had won a prize for her painting of the Peace Dome. We'd also visited Himeyuri-kan in Okinawa, a museum devoted to the student nurses who'd died when American soldiers gassed the cave-turned-hospital where they were hiding. On our last family trip to the United States, we'd stopped off in Washington D.C. where we saw the statue commemorating the American victory at Iwojima, as well as the Holocaust Memorial Museum, where I'd hurried Lilia past the exhibit about the Nazi's systematic execution of the disabled.

Lilia knows about modern wars, too. Recently she's started paying attention to TV news reports so she knows something about the French currently fighting in Mali. Two months ago, nine Japanese oil workers were taken hostage and killed by al Quaeda supporters at the Amenas gas plant in Algeria. The terrorists were reportedly acting in response to French military actions in Mali. The incident was all over Japanese TV for a couple of weeks, leading my husband to worry about our safety in Paris, but I'd already booked our hotel and paid for our plane tickets. Closer to home, North Korean leader Kim Jong Un is threatening to send a missile to South Korea or Japan or maybe the United States. That guy is on TV all the time, too.

Now, looking over the exhibits of weapons and military maps and uniforms, I try to explain about how various countries were aligned during World War II. "Japan and Germany were friends," I sign, "and France and America were allied. But now all of the countries are friends." Simple, I know, but it's about all I can manage on the spot.

Still, the evidence of war makes her sad.

We move slowly, from glass case to glass case.

"Here is the uniform the French soldiers wore in Africa," I explain. Then, later, "Here is the printing press that the French people who didn't like the Germans used to make secret newspapers."

The room is dark and there are no other visitors. At one point, the guy with short hair who'd let us in, comes to check up on us and tells us how to get to the third floor. Then he disappears again, leaving us alone.

When we reach the end, I try to remember how to get to the elevator he mentioned. Another guard appears and offers to lead us.

"She wants to see Napoleon's clothes," I say, feeling a little guilty. We're about to turn our backs to the horrors of war in order to observe fashion. How frivolous!

"*Ah, les vêtements de Napoleon,*" the man nods. "Come with me."

He asks where we are from. After I'd explained that I'm an American married to a Japanese man, living in Japan, he says, "*C'est bon ca!*" *That's good!* He then tells me about his own multicultural family. He himself is from Cote d'Ivoire. His daughter has married a Dutch national and lives in the Netherlands, and another family member has married a Vietnamese. I get caught up in his enthusiasm. We agree that marriage between people of different cultures leads to international understanding. It's very, very good!

In fact, though I often tell my children that my marriage to their father is proof of peace between our nations, they are not fully convinced. Yoshi and I don't always get along, and I think that many of our arguments are a result of cultural differences.

When we get off the elevator, the guard who first greeted us looks surprised. "Are you finished?" he asks.

Is it my imagination, or does he seem disappointed? After all, we are the only visitors so far, and we haven't even gone through the whole museum. He's obviously a member of the French military. I feel the need to apologize for our lack of interest.

"*Elle est devenue triste,*" I say, using Lilia as an excuse. And she *is* sad. Fighting between countries—or her parents—makes her miserable. "She wants to see Napoleon's things."

We say "*merci*" and "*au revoir*" and move on to another wing of les Invalides. Here, we don't need help with the elevator.

We go up with a group of gray-haired American men, whom I assume are veterans. Lilia and I look at the cases of beautiful swords with ornate hilts. One is in the form of a rooster's head. Others are in intricate filigree. We spend a meditative moment in front of Napoleon's stuffed blond horse, which is cracked from shoulder to foreleg. Finally, after going through the exhibits of Napoleon's military campaigns in Europe and North Africa, including his defeat at Waterloo, we move on to the dome which houses his tomb.

I push Lilia in a circle, trying to find the wheelchair accessible entrance. It has to be here somewhere. Most of the tourists are gathered here. Obviously, this is the most popular attraction, and there has to be an easy way inside. I decide to ask for directions at the information desk.

The young man there says, "*Je suis désolé*. That is the only place here that doesn't have a ramp."

Remembering the reactions of the guards at the Louvre, I think I'd better ask if it's okay for Lilia to go in anyway. I can help her up the stairs on my own.

The guy shows me his right elbow, which is in a cast. "I can't help you," he says.

"That's okay. I can do it."

He shrugs in typical French fashion. "Do what you like."

We go back outside. There's no railing, but from previous experience, I know that Lilia can make it up the ten or so steps with me supporting her from behind. I tell her to put the brakes on her wheelchair, unbuckle her seat belt, and stand up.

She has just taken one step when a woman offers to carry the wheelchair. I hesitate for a moment. In Japan, I have become conditioned to refuse assistance. But I need help. And she wants to help. Helping us might even make her feel happy.

"Yes, please," I say.

Then, two Middle Eastern men—Lebanese?—grab onto Lilia's arms and help her up the steps.

"*Merci beaucoup!*" I say after she is once again settled in her wheelchair. I think of all the times in Japan that we've been ignored. Sometimes people don't offer to help because it creates a never-ending chain of obligation. They think they are doing us a favor by letting us struggle on our own. I know if my husband had been with us he would have been ashamed to accept these offers of help. He would have insisted on doing everything himself in order to avoid being a burden. Although I often want to do everything by myself as an independent American woman, what I have learned from living in Japan is that sometimes it's okay to ask for help. I'm realizing that it's not a failure to accept help when it's offered. People like to help. It makes them feel good. And why not spare my aching back?

Inside the dome, it's cold. Lilia wheels herself to the center, where there's a large hole. Down at the bottom is Napoleon's tomb—a dark wooden casket, which contains coffins within coffins (six in all). Lilia grabs onto the railing and takes a photo.

"He's really in there!" she signs, awed.

"Yes!" I confirm.

I point out Empress Josephine's gray-marbled tomb, which is off to the side and up a few steps.

Lilia extracts the manga French history book from her backpack and points to the picture of Josephine.

"Yes, it's her," I say. Once again, I'm happily surprised by how much she already knows, in spite of never having had a social studies or history class.

I sit down on a bench for a while, observing the visitors from around the world. Napoleon Bonaparte was a general, a war hero, who oversaw the killing of thousands, yes, but who has also brought people together. Today, for example, the people of nations formerly at war with each other are gathered here in peace. Like us, they just want to peruse the relics of this great man, enter his tomb, pay homage, and maybe take a photo to post on Facebook. Here are all of these different people co-operating and helping each other, helping us.

When we are ready to leave, I think that it would be easiest to take Lilia,in her wheelchair, down the steps backward. It would be a bit bumpy, but I could do it on my own.

Without saying a word, a blond man—Swedish? Dutch?—picks up one side of Lilia's wheelchair and helps me carry her down the stairs.

"*Merci!*" I call after him. "Thank you!"

In this moment, I am filled with feelings of *fraternité*. For a few heartbeats, at least, it seems that we are all brothers and sisters, that there are allies everywhere.

Climbing for Camille

OVER LUNCH AT THE Café de Musée (quiche lorraine for Lilia, beef bourguignon and a glass of red wine for me), I suggest that we move on to the Rodin Museum, which is just around the corner.

As part of my effort to prepare Lilia for coming to Paris, I'd shown her several movies related to the city, including *Funny Girl*, *The Bells of Notre Dame*, *Marie Antoinette*, and the French film *Camille Claudel*, starring Gerard Depardieu as Auguste Rodin, and Isabelle Adjani as his young protégée, Camille.

Lilia shakes her head.

So much for all that pre-trip preparation. I wonder if she's tired of sightseeing, or tired of art. I, for one, have never been to the Rodin Museum. I'd been looking forward to visiting someplace new with Lilia, and I was sure that after having learned about the sculptor, she would want to go, too.

"Why not?" I ask her.

"Because of Camille," she signs.

Ah. Camille Claudel was a brilliant sculptor, and for a while, Rodin had nurtured her talent and taught her a few things. He also made her his lover. But when he moved on to somebody else, Camille went a little bit crazy. Her family had her committed, and she spent the rest of her life in a mental hospital.

After watching this film, Lilia's sympathies are with Camille. She thinks that Rodin was a boor, and that he was cruel for making his models pose in painful contortions for hours on end. Lilia has a strong sense of social justice, which makes me proud. I'd thought that in showing her the movie, I was giving her a lesson in art history, but Lilia latched onto something else. She is more concerned with how the people in the film treated each other. Maybe she has learned the right lesson after all.

During our flight, I'd read in a French magazine that a new film about Claudel was debuting; this one starred Juliet Binoche as the artist and was a story about a three-day period of her stay in the mental hospital. Though I'd thought briefly about taking Lilia to see it, I now knew it was a bad idea. It would just make her feel sad.

"Camille's works are in the museum, too," I tell Lilia now. "Don't you want to see *her* sculptures?"

She nods. *Good.* We're back on track.

I sop up the last of my beef stew with crusty French bread, and Lilia polishes off her salad. We venture back out onto the street. The sun shines overhead, and Lilia's silk scarf flaps in the gentle breeze. Down a cobble-stoned side street, just before the museum entrance, we come across a pole adorned with round blue and red stickers. It reminds me of Yayoi Kusama's polka dot art. Upon closer inspection, I find that the stickers are proof of admittance to the museum. Apparently, someone established the custom of peeling the stickers off after touring the museum and plastering them to this pole: a community art project.

At the front door of the museum, we are waved inside. No one bothers to ask for proof of Lilia's disability as they do in Japan. Even when it's clear that she uses a wheelchair and that she can't stand or walk, museum and theater attendants back home always insist upon seeing the little red booklet that makes her disabilities official. I like that the French are more casual and easy-going about wheelchair users. We are admitted to a temporary exhibit of Rodin's work in a gallery off the lobby. Pale marble sculptures are arranged on either side of a long ramp. At first Lilia is diffident, but she gradually becomes interested in the hands and heads and bodies, sometimes imitating the uncomfortable positions of the figures.

There are numerous sculptures in the gallery of the great French writer Victor Hugo: not only his head, with its full beard and wild mane, but also his naked body. I later read that Hugo did not actually pose in the nude for Rodin. In fact, he was already dead in 1889 when the sculptor received a commission from the Third Republic to create a monument to his idol. Rodin had initially been prompted to sculpt Hugo after critics, finding his work too realistic, had accused him of casting his brilliant *The Age of Bronze* from life. His supporter, the journalist Edmond Bazire, suggested that he create a portrait of a prominent figure such as Victor Hugo, who would never consent to having his face cast, in order to lay suspicions to rest.

Lilia, too, finds the nudes overly realistic. "*Hazukashii*," she says, averting her eyes. *Embarrassing.*

We go out into the garden where many of Rodin's most famous works are on display, including *The Thinker*, which sits atop the sculptor's grave, surrounded by topiary. There is a replica of this sculpture of a man sitting with his chin in hand, elbow on knee, in front of the Kinokuniya bookstore at the mall near our house in Japan. I've also seen a rendition at an art museum in Tokyo. Everyone in Japan, including my kids, knows this sculpture even if they don't know the artist's name.

I read that back in the day, a lot of people didn't know what to make of Rodin. The fashion at the time was to sculpt idealized images of the human body for decorative purposes. Rodin was more interested in portraying the body as it really was, in the belief that an observer could understand a subject's character through his or her gestures and expressions. He sometimes sculpted only part of a body: a hand, for example, and considered it finished.

"Is it broken?" Lilia asks me, gesturing to the headless "Walking Man."

"No, he didn't make a head to begin with," I tell her.

She nods, thoughtfully.

At the far end of the garden, we come across a gushing fountain. Before entering the pale yellow building which houses some of the smaller sculptures, Lilia wants to sketch, so I settle on a bench to watch and wait.

I imagine being here before all the sculptures were positioned among the sketchy winter trees, back when Rodin wandered these grounds along with other guests of the Hotel Biron. At that time, it was a veritable artist's colony, having housed such luminous tenants as writer Jean Cocteau, painter and paper cutter Henri Matisse, poet Rainer Maria Rilke, and dancer Isadora Duncan. The hotel, with its filigreed black iron balcony, is now part of the Rodin Museum. After Lilia finishes her sketch of the fountain and we explore the garden a bit more, I push her up the ramp to the pale yellow townhouse.

On the first floor, I'm surprised to come across a sculpted woman's head with Japanese features and a geisha-style topknot. "Look," I indicate to Lilia. "Her name was 'Hanako.'" I later find out that Hanako was the stage name of Hisa Ota, an actress and dancer trained as a geisha, and that Rodin had planned to use her as a model for a bust of Beethoven, of all people. He modeled 58 sculptures of Hanako, and sketched her countless times, often drawing without looking at the paper, keeping his eyes on his subject.

Unfortunately, there are no sculptures by Camille Claudel on the first floor, and there's no elevator to the second floor. I gesture to the majestic winding marble staircase with its wrought iron railing and explain to Lilia.

"Shall we forget about it?" I try to convey that it's all right with me if we don't see every nook and cranny of the museum. Sure, I would love to take a look at Camille's work, but this trip is for Lilia. I don't want her to feel bad about not being able to get up the stairs. I figure it's better to make light of it. It's not her fault that the second floor is inaccessible by wheelchair.

Lilia takes a long look at the steps that seem to go all the way to the sky. Then, with a look of resolve, she points up. "*Ikkitai*! I can do it!"

I bite my lip. It's a long way. Then again, maybe she really can make it all the way up. I'll give her a hand, and she can always plop down on the marble steps and take a break if she needs to. Who cares if people stare? We stand out in Japan, as well. We're used to it. Or I am, at least. And besides, she's been climbing a similar set of stairs almost every day over the past school year. What was that training for, if not occasions like this one?

"Okay! Let's do it!" Remembering again how particular the guards had been at the Louvre, I think it best to check in with the staff before we haul the wheelchair up. I approach a guy behind the desk near the entrance.

"I know there's no elevator," I say, "but is it okay if we go up? She can climb a bit, and I'll help her."

He gives me a Gallic shrug. "*Oui*. Go ahead."

I position Lilia's wheelchair near the handrail at an angle and help her get to her feet. She grips the railing with one hand, I grab the other, and she begins to climb, positioning her feet slowly and deliberately, like someone marching underwater.

Perhaps inspired by Lilia's heroic effort, the guy rushes from behind the desk and offers to carry her wheelchair to the top of the stairs.

"*Oui, merci!*" By now, I no longer hesitate. I'm happy to accept help whenever we need it. This museum is not completely accessible, and I am done with being a martyr.

We rise slowly, step by step, without taking a break. Even I'm a bit winded by the time we reach the top. Lilia, who has climbed all the way with her legs bent at the knees sinks into her chair and signs, "I'm tired!"

"You did a great job! I'm proud of you!"

Lilia catches her breath and we find Camille's head wrapped in cloth, as sculpted by Rodin, which we both recognize from the movie. And there is *L'Âge Mûr,* in which a kneeling naked young woman reaches toward an old man who is in the embrace of an elderly woman. This sculpture was interpreted as being a depiction of Camille's yearning for Rodin. Her famous head of Rodin with its unruly bronze beard is also there, as is *The Waltz*. Camille worked on a smaller scale. No one ever accused her of taking casts of bodies. Like Rodin's, her works are full of emotion, but with more grace.

Lilia circles the sculptures, studying them, memorizing them. Finally, satisfied, we go back down the steps.

ON THE WAY BACK to our hotel, we add our museum stickers to the pole and then stop at a chocolatier, Herve Chavin, to observe another kind of sculpting. The window is filled with Easter candy as exquisite as art: a large, filigreed chocolate egg, finely detailed rabbits, and chicks.

Once inside we're drawn to the glass case of perfectly formed macarons in many colors. Lilia and I had tried to make them ourselves a couple of weeks before, so we know how fussy they are; you have to beat the egg whites to just the right consistency, you have to bang the pan three times when it comes out of the oven, etc.; how difficult, and how delicious. We select a few flavors: raspberry, chocolate, the intriguing basil, and yuzu, a Japanese citrus fruit that is often floated in the bath in winter.

Back in our apartment, I heat water and pour it over flowers that I bought at a Japanese tea shop and tucked into my suitcase. I thought it would remind Lilia of the scene in *Marie Antoinette* when the princess serves her visiting brother peony tea from China. But Lilia declines a cup. "I don't like hot tea," she signs. She watches the petals unfurl, and bites into a macaron. Although I'm a little disappointed that she has declined to take even a sip, I let it go and drink both cups myself.

THAT EVENING, Lilia and I have reservations for a show at the Japan Culture Center which is prominently situated near the Eiffel Tower. The theater company Derashinera is presenting *Game* featuring Japanese mime Shûji Onodera, which seems to be the perfect blend of East and West for Lilia and me. We will be able to enjoy the play without subtitles or interpretation, without any special assistance at all.

We change into dresses—Lilia in her purple tiered dress, and me in a black dress and duster. I wear new black shoes; not spiky ones, but shoes that I know I can walk well in. And then we go across the street to catch a taxi.

There are no cabs at the taxi stand. We wait, and wait. I know where the Culture Center is since we passed it on the way to the hotel from the airport, and again from the Louvre. It's not that far. If we could hop into a car, we'd be there in a few minutes, but all the taxis seem to be occupied.

I look at my watch. We're running out of time. Well, maybe if we head in the direction of the Eiffel Tower, we'll be able to flag a cab down on the way. I abandon our wait and start pushing Lilia's wheelchair.

I walk fast, clip-clopping down the sidewalk, ignoring the blisters bubbling on my feet, the sweat sheening my forehead. When we push through the glass doors of the ultra-modern Culture Center I'm happy to see that we have ten minutes to spare. Since we already have reservations, we don't need to wait in line to buy tickets. An usher escorts us to an elevator, reaches inside and pushes a button.

"Someone will be waiting for you when you get off," he says.

The elevator stops. We enter a room which is dark, except for a dimly lit rock garden. No one is there. We wait for a few minutes, but no one comes. I try the door. Lilia scolds me. We watch the elevators going up and down. We wait some more. I check the time on my phone. By now, the performance is underway. I begin to think we are in some absurdist play ourselves. I laugh to myself. Finally, I hear footsteps clattering on the floor below, where the administrative offices are located.

"Wait," I sign to Lilia, with the back of a hand under my chin. What else could she do?

I dash down the stairs. *"Pardon? Pardon?"*

A man appears.

"Where is the play?" I ask. "We were sent here, but..."

"It's not here."

"Évidemment."

He leads us back onto the elevator and we are taken to the second-floor balcony, the right place, where an usher quickly shows us to the wheelchair accessible seats which are behind a latticed railing. Our view is obstructed. I can take in the entire stage only if I lean way down and to the side. Someone in a rabbit costume comes onstage, and then an alarm clock goes off, and then later, actors wearing pig masks, playing some kind of card game.

If we'd entered the theater before the show had started, we could have gotten ourselves into the regular seats, with an unobstructed view. But the performance—a mixture of modern dance, mime, and theater - is witty and captivating. Since it's not a typical stage play, it doesn't matter so much that we missed the very beginning. We finally are here, where we wanted to be, anyway. Lilia laughs and claps, and I ignore the crick in my neck and begin to relax.

Afterwards, I don't bother trying to flag down a taxi. In my fancy clothes, I push Lilia's wheelchair at a more leisurely pace past the Subway Sandwich shop, past the doors with Arabic writing, past the Monoprix, all the way to our apart-hotel.

When we are at last back in our room in our pajamas, I ask Lilia "Where do you want to go next?"

"To Versailles!"

Lilia in the Metro or A Visit to Versailles

I KNOW THAT Sunday isn't the best day for a visit to one of France's premier tourist attractions. The website suggests that it will be mobbed, and I'm worried about the weather. If it's sunny, or at least not raining, we will go. The question is how to get there?

Originally, I had planned on going by taxi or hiring a guide for door-to-door service. But I don't really want a guided a tour. Without Japanese Sign Language, or at least Japanese, Lilia wouldn't be able to understand anyway. And the metro would be way cheaper than taking a taxi.

By day three I'm feeling more confident about our ability to get around. I noticed an elevator at the Bir Hakeim train station, and I discovered that many of the major metro stations are wheelchair accessible. Line 14 is fully accessible, in accordance with new French laws. And, if nothing else, the metro will be an essential Parisian experience.

After a leisurely breakfast of *pain au chocolat,* sliced pears, and ham, I push the wheelchair down the street toward the Eiffel Tower and the Bir Hakeim train station. I'd assumed that metro maps for wheelchair users would be available throughout Paris, but that's not the case. After standing before the ticket vending machine for a few minutes, trying to figure out how to buy a ticket to Versailles with my credit card, I give up and go to the window.

You have heard that the French are rude to tourists—I have written it here myself—but the guy in the ticket window has infinite patience. Even though there is a line growing behind me, he remains calm when I can't remember my PIN number. He comes out from behind the booth and helps me buy tickets from the vending machine, then he draws our route on a map. We'll have to change trains a couple of times to get onto Line 14. When I can't figure out how to get through the gate to the elevator, even though the directions are written clearly on a sign (Silly me! I didn't read the sign!), he helps us through the gate, all the while maintaining perfect composure.

I realize that maybe I am becoming a little bit too dependent upon the kindness of strangers. There was a time when I would have been able to figure everything out all by myself. Special treatment because of Lilia's wheelchair is making me soft. Or maybe it's just because I've spent so many years living in Japan where people are always quick to help hapless foreigners, where as soon as I open a map, a stranger will offer to show me the way. Then again, bringing my daughter to France was something of an accomplishment, wasn't it? And accepting assistance when I need it isn't such a bad thing.

Lilia has been to cities with underground railways before—Tokyo, Osaka, Washington D.C.—but this will be her first-ever ride on a subway. I maneuver her wheelchair onto the metro car. Knees move aside to make room. Lilia puts on her brakes and the train surges toward the next station. Opposite us, an older woman sits, eyes downcast. A young mother wrangles with her small child. A group of brightly dressed tourists (Americans?) cling to the poles.

We are all absorbed with our own thoughts, thinking ahead, perhaps, to a day at work, a playdate, a morning of sightseeing. Just then, a shaggy-haired guy, with a guitar slung over his shoulder, steps into the car. Great. There goes my peace and quiet. And he'll probably come around with a cup, asking for money.

Lilia eyes him with curiosity. This is something totally new to her. Although I've seen street performers in Tokyo, and even in front of the Tokushima train station, there are signs in the Japanese subway system prohibiting buskers. He begins to strum. Lilia starts to nod and clap along with him. Realizing that he has an audience, he sings directly to her, a serenade to my thirteen-year-old daughter. I fight the urge to still her hands and divert her attention.

The older woman across from us smiles at her, and so does the harried young mother. I give in to the moment, until a grin spreads across my face as well.

At the next stop, the man crosses the car and says something to Lilia before getting off. He doesn't know that she can't hear him. We don't give him any money; he doesn't ask for any. "Au revoir," Lilia says, waving and waving until he is out of sight.

We get off at the following stop. So now we have to find the correct exit and our next metro. We go to the end of the platform to find stairs. We go to the other end...more stairs. Now I'm confused. Hadn't the guy at Bir Hakeim shown us an accessible route? Does "accessible" mean something different to the French? If we go up the wrong steps, we'll have to come back down. And what if I made a mistake, and we got off at the wrong stop entirely? There's no one around to ask. I have a horrible vision of being stuck in the metro for hours: a version of hell.

I finally make a decision. We'll try the shorter of the two staircases.

"Can you climb up those steps?" I ask Lilia. There are only about five, and there's a railing that she can hang on to.

She nods. Well, she managed the staircase at the Hotel Biron. This will be cake. She gets out of her wheelchair and grabs onto the railing. I carry the wheelchair up to the top and set it down at an angle so she'll be able to sit down. At the top, we find the stairs to the next platform. It's a busier stop, and lots of commuters are bustling past us. There are more stairs than before, but going down is always easier than going up.

I park the wheelchair at the top of the stairs. "Ready?" I ask.

Lilia nods gamely.

But just before she's about to get up again, a pair of young men rush over and volunteer to help. It all happens so fast. They heft Lilia and her wheelchair like an ancient empress's palanquin and deposit her safely at the bottom of the steps.

"*Merci!*" I call after them. "*Merci beaucoup!*"

In the train station, I find a woman worker and ask for help. She tells me that the elevator to the platform we need isn't working. The train will have to be diverted to another track, but she and another worker will help us board.

"She'll have to step down at Versailles," the woman warns.

"She can do that," I say. "I'll help her."

When it's time to board, the workers set up a gangway going from the platform to the train. Steps lead up or down to the seats, so we'll have to wait near the door. There's no place for me to sit. Oh, well. It might be uncomfortable for a little while, but it's cheaper than taking a taxi or a private tour. Plus, it's an adventure.

At the stop for Versailles, another kind Frenchman helps us off the train and shows us to the slightly difficult-to-find ramp that leads out of the station. Then, after what seems like hours underground and enclosed, we step into the chilly, spring day.

To find our way to the palace, all we have to do is follow the hordes. People from all over the world—China, Japan, America, and from other European countries speaking languages I can't identify—are surging toward Versailles. If this is the off-season, I hate to imagine how crowded it would be during a Sunday in high season.

We pass a street performer: a guy dressed like an Egyptian mummy. His skin is golden, his eyes dramatically outlined. And he is as stoic as those British guys in bear hats outside Buckingham Palace. A bucket for coins is positioned in front of him.

When we get to the gates of Versailles, a guard directs us to the entrance for the disabled. We bump over the cobblestones, past long lines of tourists waiting to get in. And then finally, we are inside.

"*Tabetai*," Lilia signs. *I'm hungry.*

It's already noon, but the only food I can find are the macarons at the Laduree shop near the entrance. *"Let them eat cake!"* Tempting, but we need something more substantial. To get to the restaurants, we'll have to go through the palace first.

"Can you wait just a little while?" I ask her.

She nods.

Because we have recently watched Sophia Coppola's *Marie Antoinette*, in which Kirsten Dunst, as the queen, runs down deserted corridors, I find the large number of visitors disconcerting. I'd somehow imagined Lilia and me alone, in the Hall of 578 Mirrors, reflected ad infinitum, or wandering the gardens quietly instead of trying to stay out of other people's snapshots. The Hall of Mirrors, created in 1686, once represented the economic and cultural power of France and the society of the royal court where seeing and being seen, preferably in one's most gorgeous gown, were so important. On this day, however, the mirrors multiply hordes of tourists. If we want to see anything at all, we'll have to fight our way to the front.

Lilia doesn't seem bothered by the crush of humanity or the disconnect between fantasy and reality. She doesn't seem to overly mind her wheelchair-level view of hundreds of bottoms from around the world. *Au contraire.* She looks up, up, up and notices the painted ceilings, which are indeed splendid. Glittery chandeliers drip down and images of well-fed angels floating on billowy clouds are framed in gilt, along with full-color scenes celebrating the first years of the reign of Louis XIV.

Luckily, there are attentive docents, mostly young men, on hand down below. Whenever one of them sees Lilia's wheelchair, he creates a path to the main attraction. Lilia gets a good look at Marie Antoinette's bed with its floral tapestry cover, which she recognizes from the movie, and the table where the King and Queen publicly dined.

By the time we've seen the requisite sites and posed for the obligatory photo in the Hall of Mirrors, we are faint with hunger. We head for Angelina's for *croque monsieur* sandwiches and its trademark African hot chocolate. (A little history: Angelina's was once called Rumpelmayers. It was once a favorite hang-out of Audrey Hepburn and Coco Chanel.)

The hot chocolate, so rich and thick that you could almost eat it with a fork, comes with a generous side dish of whipped cream. Although one website warned that the wait staff at Angelina's Tea Room doesn't speak much English, our waiter is fluent. I even hear him speaking Japanese to the two guys at the next table.

After lunch, we take a little train past grazing sheep in green pastures and visitors on bicycles to le Grand Trianon. Napoleon Bonaparte once made this his residence, as did Charles de Gaulle. The crowd is thinner here so we're able to wander more freely. Lilia sets herself up in front of the ornate gate and begins sketching.

Once inside, we're permitted to go beyond the velvet ropes of one room, while other tourists snap photos from behind the barrier. I wonder how many strangers' photo albums we will appear in.

We still haven't gotten to La Petite Trianon, Marie Antoinette's playhouse, but it's getting late and I'm tired. We have to take the train and subway back to Paris and I want to save a little bit of energy.

"Is it okay if we go back to the hotel?" I ask Lilia.

She nods, but I can tell she's a little disappointed.

"We'll come again," I tell her. "We'll see Marie Antoinette's house next time." Having made it this far, another visit no longer seems outside the realm of possibility.

We get back on the little train and return to the palace where we take a few final photos of the gushing fountains and the sprawling lawn. And then I push Lilia back down the hill, over the bumpy cobblestones, and through the gauntlet of Africans selling Eiffel Tower keychains. The street performer dressed as an Egyptian mummy is still there, outside the gates. As far as I can tell, he's been there all day, in the exact same position. Impressive.

"Here." I hand Lilia a euro. "Put this in the bucket."

She rolls over to the performer and drops the coin in with the others, then poses for a photo. The "mummy" doesn't move.

I wonder how long he will stay here. Maybe he's been coming every day for years. Maybe someday I'll finally find a full-time job in Japan and we'll have enough money to come back to this place, to check out the rest of Versailles, and this street performer will still be here.

Boys and *Un Bateau*

LILIA HAS DECIDED that French guys are "*ikemen*," a Japanese word meaning something like "hot" or "cool." After a particularly adorable young man with big brown eyes sees me struggling to get Lilia up the escalator and steps in to help out, she declares that she wants to come back to live in France and marry a Parisian. If you can find a guy like that, go for it, I think. He'd been not only super-cute, but also super-kind, lamenting the lack of accessibility in this newest of metro stations. "Don't wait for someone to come and offer to help you," he chides. "People here are kind."

By the time we get back to our hotel, I'm worn out. Lilia has gone all Marie Antoinette on me, and is insisting that I push her everywhere, despite her perfectly good arms, which are perfectly capable of propelling the wheelchair. Whenever I ask her to do it herself, if only for a few meters, she throws out her hands as if she's tossing breadcrumbs to the pigeons at her feet, in the sign for "I'm tired."

For our next big trip, to Rouen on Tuesday, I decide that I will go ahead and ask for help, as Big Brown Eyes had suggested. I grab my tablet and do an internet search for "wheelchair tours in Paris." I come across an American expat who specializes in just that. No rates are listed on the website, but previous customers offer glowing testimonials. The man knows which metro and train stations are accessible. He pushes the wheelchair. He handles everything so that able-bodied accompaniers can wander around freely, without having to keep an eye out for curb cuts. The cost for a tour would no doubt put us over our 100 euro per diem, but who cares? I have a credit card. And my shoulders are starting to ache.

I dash off an email. And wait.

This guy seems pretty popular, and it occurs to me that I should have made reservations well in advance, not two days before I need his services. But I've overestimated Lilia's stamina, and who knew that I would be so tired?

Next, I update my Facebook page. One of my friends has added a comment to the previous day's post, worrying about "the riots" in Paris. What? We've been in a bubble of blissful ignorance. I haven't picked up a newspaper since *Le Figaro* on the airplane. And I haven't turned on the television since "Le Famille Cromagnon." I do another quick Internet search and discover that while we were checking out Marie Antoinette's bedroom and sipping African hot chocolate at Angelina's, there had been a huge demonstration on les Champs-Élysées to protest a French bill about to be put to vote legalizing gay marriage. Hundreds of thousands assembled, and dozens were arrested. The police employed tear gas and batons.

I don't mention any of this to Lilia. Although it occurs to me that this is a teachable moment, I don't want anything to destroy her dream of Paris. So far, most of the people we've met have been very kind and helpful. For now, at least, I'll let her believe that everyone here lives in harmony, that tolerance reigns supreme.

After our big excursion to Versailles, we need a little break. On Monday, we hang around our hotel room until noon. "Ready for lunch?" I ask Lilia.

She nods.

I want her to sample the basics of French cuisine. Just as

we have a list of must-see locations and activities (next up: a ride on *un bateau mouche*, and a visit to Notre Dame) I have a culinary checklist in my head:

Quiche Lorraine: Check!

Beef Bourguignon: Check!

Pain au chocolat: Check!

Croque Monsieur: Check!

I also want Lilia to try pizza, of the authentic Mediterranean variety. Back when I was a student, my favorite French pizza had been one with a thin crust and an egg cooked over easy on top—a revelation after a childhood of Gino's frozen pizzas and Domino's. Lilia was more used to my homemade Chicago-style deep dish pizza or the Japanese varieties delivered by the local Pizza Royal Hat—German potato special (which came with a choice of Italian or curry sauce), seaweed and yogurt, or the chicken teriyaki pizza.

We stop by Carmine, a pizzeria with a dark-paneled interior near our hotel. As soon as we're in the door, a young French ponytailed waiter takes in the wheelchair, and without much fuss, settles us at a small table next to a couple of businessmen on their noon break.

I study the menu. The closest thing to the pizza that I remember is the Iberian. I order one of those for myself, and after consulting Lilia, a Margherita for her.

"Why don't you order from the child's menu for your daughter?" the waiter suggests in English.

"Well, she's thirteen." The child's menu is for kids up to twelve, and sure, she is small, but Lilia can put away a lot of food. I don't want to break any rules or take advantage.

He shrugs. "The adult pizza is too big and too expensive. Plus, the child's comes with fruit and salad."

Well, if he's willing to bend the rules, then fine. "Okay."

Lilia wants fries, too. The businessmen next to us have a big serving of them, and they look delicious.

"And, um, *des pommes frites, s'il vous plait.*"

Our waiter gives me a dubious frown as he adds that to

our order. He seems pretty sure that we won't be able to eat everything, or maybe he thinks we're being pigs. And maybe he's right, I think, as another waiter brings our neighbors an enormous serving of *tarte tatin* for dessert. This place is not about skimpy servings.

Soon our order arrives. My pizza is indeed platter-sized. Lilia's is slightly smaller, but yes, there are heaps of food on the table and it's all delicious. The pizza crust is perfectly crisp, the sauce delicately seasoned with fresh herbs, and the egg on my Iberian is just as I recall. We eat as much as we can, guiltily leaving a few golden fries behind.

After lunch, I check out the lavatory. Happily, it is accessible, so I wheel Lilia inside. When we emerge, our *ikemen* waiter is standing there with our coats. We haven't paid yet, and I'm sure that he knows, but he takes charge of Lilia's wheelchair and hustles us out the door. I take out my wallet.

"Which way are you going?" he asks, ignoring my gesture.

I point in the direction of the Seine.

He positions Lilia's wheelchair and shakes her hand. "*Au revoir*!"

I stand there for a moment, baffled, wondering if I should run back inside and try to pay the bill. Maybe we shouldn't be accepting charity. Maybe it's giving Lilia the wrong idea. We aren't like those people sitting on the side of the road waiting for hand-outs. We're prepared to pay for services. But then again, maybe our waiter was being kind. Maybe he'd been charmed by our mother-daughter duo, and it would be churlish to refuse this gift. We shout "*Merci! Merci beaucoup!*" and proceed on our way.

He smiles and waves.

IT'S A BRISK twenty-minute walk to the docks of the famous Bateaux Mouches. As I push Lilia's wheelchair down the sidewalk, careful to avoid doggy-doo, we see a woman "walking" a trio of white Pomeranians without a leash. We see another dog in a flower shop, and a Husky peering into a restaurant with its perfectly coiffed middle-aged woman owner. Lilia loves dogs, so this is one of the benefits of traveling through the city above ground, on foot—or wheels.

From walking, we also learn that the French are much more lax about jaywalking than the Japanese. Pedestrians cross the street whether the light is green or not. In Japan, this would be dangerous. Suicidal, even. Japanese drivers are prone to run red lights, and I've rarely seen anyone stop for pedestrians waiting at a crosswalk, even next to my son's school. I don't want Lilia to forget about traffic safety, so we stop and wait on the curb when the light is red. We watch the Parisians ignore the signal and go across. When the light finally turns green, Lilia raises her hand, as she was taught in Japan, so drivers will be sure to see her in spite of her small stature.

At the docks for the bateaux mouches there are plenty of ramps. I buy our tickets and we board without much fanfare, taking seats on the deck. Among our fellow passengers are a group of Chinese tourists. One woman wears rhinestone-studded boots and a pink scarf. As the cruise gets underway, she has her photo taken in front of nearly every monument.

The boat chugs along the Seine, making a loop around Île de la Cité, which once constituted the whole of Paris, and which is now, most notably, home to Notre Dame. We pass the Maison de la Culture Japonaise, where we'd seen the Japanese mime, the Eiffel Tower, and the Institut du Monde Arabe. From this perspective the bridges are varied and beautiful. We glide under the Pont de Bir Hakeim with its ornate stone carvings, the Pont d'Alma which will forever be associated in my mind with the death of Princess Diana, the Pont d'Alexandre III, which is as extravagant as a wedding cake. And the Pont des Arts, adorned with lovers' padlocks. Seagulls wheel and dip over the water behind us. Houseboats bob gently in our wake.

Lilia takes out her sketchbook and begins to draw. After I point out the Conciergerie, which served as a prison during the French Revolution, she pencils a silhouette of Marie

Antoinette. I try once or twice to draw her attention to the other buildings and monuments, but then give up. I don't want to be a nag. And besides, it's better to relax and enjoy the ride. Lilia is enjoying herself.

After our cruise, I'm sure we'll be able to hop into a taxi right outside. Or maybe a tuk-tuk. But I can see nothing but tour buses. There aren't even any Africans selling Eiffel Tower keychains. I gaze up the steep incline and sigh. Okay, okay. At least I'll be working off some of that pizza.

We finally flag down a taxi and direct the driver to take us to Notre Dame, which Lilia knows from the animated Disney movie, "The Bells of Notre Dame." The church, with its lace-like stone work, is surrounded by people. Some are waiting to get inside, some are just hanging out, enjoying the late afternoon sunshine. On the first floor of the cathedral, worshippers are crowded into simple wooden pews. Chandeliers hang between stone pillars leading up to the altar. Light streams through the stained-glass windows. I don't let on that there are stairs going to the top for a close-up view of the gargoyles. We wouldn't be able to manage those anyhow.

Lilia asks about the votive candles lit around the statues of various saints.

"You can light one for someone that you want to pray for," I tell her. "Do you want to light a candle?"

She nods. I give her a euro to tuck into the money box, and hand her a candle.

"I'm praying for the health of Grandma and Grandpa in America, and *Obaachan* in Japan," she signs. She lights the candle, put her hands together, and closes her eyes for a moment.

Lilia gives another euro to the elderly nun at the door, who sits collecting coins.

After leaving the church, we pause to watch a street performer blow soap bubbles bigger than our heads. Over the bridge, there is a row of souvenir shops crammed with T-shirts, paperweights, and postcards, among other things. I buy a baseball decorated with images of Paris for Jio, boxer shorts with a Parisian motif for Yoshi, and an apron for my sister-in-law; then we drop by Shakespeare and Company, the famous used English-language bookstore and flophouse. A reading is in progress, so we don't go inside, but we browse the used books on display on the sidewalk before taking a taxi back to our hotel.

I check my email, hoping there is a reply from the wheelchair tour guide saying that he was able to pencil us in on extremely short notice. But there's nothing. If we are going to Rouen in the morning, I'll have to get us there on my own.

Joan of Arc and the Heart

BY DAY FOUR, Lilia and I are starting to get snippy with each other. The novelty of being in Paris has worn off slightly, and once again I am urging her to wash her face, brush her teeth, and put on her shoes. We have a big day ahead of us, but she is sitting at the desk in her pajamas playing World of Goo on my tablet, which I've brought along for e-mail and research.

"Hurry up!" I sign. "We have to get to the train station! It'll take us a long time to get to Rouen."

Lilia sighs and reluctantly closes the window on the tablet. Slowly, slowly, she begins to change her clothes while I consult the guidebook one more time.

There are various locations associated with Joan of Arc in France: Domrémy-la-Pucelle, where she was born in about 1412, and where she, an illiterate twelve-year-old peasant girl, allegedly received heavenly visions charging her with the duty to drive the marauding English occupiers out of France and lead the Dauphin to Reims; Tours, where she met Charles VII, who became her supporter, at the Chateau de Chinon; Reims, where she attended the coronation of King Charles VII; and Orleans, where she led an army to victory at the age of nineteen. One of the closest related sites is Rouen, an hour and a half by train from Paris, where she was imprisoned and burned at the stake for heresy.

When we are finally dressed and out the door, we take a taxi to the bustling Gare St. Lazarre. Once inside, we gaze around for a moment before a kind gentleman approaches us and offers assistance. He is, as it turns out, an employee of SNCF, the French railroad, and he knows exactly where we need to go. He shows us to an office at the other end of the building and tells the guy at the desk that we need help getting on and off the train. Easy peasy.

I can also buy our tickets here.

"How old is she?" the guy asks.

"Thirteen," I say.

"If she were twelve, she would be eligible for a lower fare...."

But she is almost fourteen. I'm not going to lie.

He hesitates for a moment, then tells me that he's going to charge me for one adult ticket and one child's ticket. We sit and wait in the quiet office, away from the jostling commuters, until it's time to board.

A couple of young women in SNCF uniforms get us settled in the accessible compartment. The purple plush seats are new and clean and comfortable, a far cry from sitting on the dirty steps of the train to Versailles. There is even a wheelchair-accessible toilet.

In Rouen, there are more railway workers waiting to help us get off and into the station. The town itself is small, medieval, and charming. The surrounding houses are made of stone. Our first order of business is to find some lunch.

We exit the station and step into one of the first viable restaurants we come across: La Metropole, with its red awning and wide windows. The tables are close together, and it's a tight fit with the wheelchair, but we manage. Some businessmen are speaking English at the next table. A pregnant French woman is dining alone. When I open the menu, I read that this place was once a favorite of Simone de Beauvoir and Jean-Paul Sartre. Simone often waited here for Jean-Paul to finish up his classes at the local university. I'd already decided that I wouldn't drag Lilia to famous hangouts of French or expat writers, which would have little meaning for her. Back in Japan, we'd decided that the theme of our travels would be history and art. But I'm delighted to have stumbled across a literary landmark anyhow. Although I have some issues with how Simone conducted herself in her relationship with Jean-Paul, she is an icon, and her novel *The Blood of Others,* about the French Resistance, is one of my all-time favorite books.

Lilia is momentarily impressed when I explain that a writer I admire has dined here.

"Do you know her?" she asks. "Is she your friend?"

Lilia knows that many of my friends are writers; she's seen their photos on book jackets after meeting them in person, so this is not an altogether ridiculous question.

"No, she lived a long time ago," I say, although I would like to have met her. "She was very famous. I just read her books."

AT LUNCH, Lilia becomes irritated when I suggest she wipe the tomato sauce from her mouth. Once back on the sidewalk, I become exasperated with her for not wheeling herself. By now my shoulders are aching from pushing her all over Paris, yet having gone over our per diem the past two days, I'm reluctant to take any more cabs. I also find her level of enthusiasm insufficient. After all, it would have been easier to hang out in Paris, maybe visit the Orsay Museum, than to schlep all the way to Normandy. We also fight over the camera. Lilia wants to be in charge of taking pictures, but I want to make sure that I get some publishable photos in case I sell a travel essay on this expedition.

We follow a sign down a cobbled side street and come across the gray-stoned dungeon where Joan was imprisoned during her last days. It isn't open to tourists today, which is just as well, because I'd read that there are only stairs leading to the chamber where she was kept. We stand for a few minutes looking up at the conical tower, trying to imagine being trapped inside without any windows, without any hope.

Most historians agree that Joan's trial was politically motivated, and that her trial was unfair. Although she was arrested for heresy, the charge was not considered a capital offense unless it was repeated. And while cross-dressing was a crime back then, she only wore men's clothing and kept her hair short so as to avoid molestation, not because she wanted to be a boy. She wasn't a feminist, either. She was simply trying to obey God while keeping her virtue intact. According the laws of the time, she should have been guarded by nuns. She was guarded by English males, instead, and at least one of them tried to rape her.

Historians who've studied the court transcripts have remarked upon her intelligence. She had no education, but she did great things. Although I can't imagine my own children going off in a few years to meet kings and lead armies, and although I know that Joan is still discussed six hundred years after her birth because she was so exceptional, I can't help but be encouraged by her humble beginnings. My daughter may read at only an almost third grade level, but Joan couldn't read at all.

After taking a few requisite photos, we move on. We find the Rouen Cathedral, which dates from the 11th century, and figures in the background of at least one painting of Joan's death. Although Lilia and I don't go inside, I find out later that the heart of Richard the Lionhearted is entombed inside, as well as the entire body of John Lancaster, Duke of Bedford, who is considered to be Joan of Arc's murderer.

Perhaps from paintings, I have this vague idea that Joan was burned at the stake right in front of this cathedral. However, there are no markers or monuments to indicate the exact site. Also, there is no Joan of Arc paraphernalia in the gift shop just adjacent to the square.

At the shop, I buy a guide to Rouen in Japanese, to the confusion of the young man at the cash register. Clearly, I am an English-speaking American, not a Japanese tourist. "For my daughter," I explain, and ask where Joan was executed.

He draws me a little map.

Meanwhile, Lilia seems more interested in window shopping at the H & M off the square, or stopping for a snack. I'm trying to find the Eglise de Jean d'Arc, while she is bugging me for a drink. We're supposed to be supplanting Lilia's education.

"We need to find the place where she died!" I insist. We need to pay homage to this amazing, brave young woman. Why should we care, in this moment, about the latest fashions? I charge on.

We pass a man in a wheelchair parked against a stone wall. A cup for coins is at his feet. Lilia looks at me as if she is expecting an explanation. At home in our living room, I am always drawing her attention to people in wheelchairs on TV: "Lilia, look at them, playing wheelchair basketball!" or "Lilia, look at the woman wheeling herself across the desert of Australia!" But this time, I'd rather move on. I shake my head and push her onward. I don't want her to imagine that this man represents her future.

We pass beneath a gilded clock and look in windows full of Easter chocolate—rabbits on skis, Pingu with a fish in his mouth—and macarons in many flavors. We go by another shop selling candy flower bouquets and Hello Kitty lollipops. And then we come to the Tears of Our Lady of Rouen Bakery. I figure "Our Lady" refers to Joan. We must be getting closer.

And there it is: a simple wooden cross rising into the air. A sign declaring, "Le Bucher. The location where Joan of Arc was burnt May 30th 1431." It's humble, like Joan herself. Lilia gasps with surprise and remarks that she was born on May 30, the anniversary of the day that Joan died—a cosmic connection. We throw our heads back, look up at the cross, and have a moment of silence.

To sweeten our sorrow, we indulge in Nutella crepes, and return to the square. By the time we finally go into the H & M near the cathedral, Lilia has mellowed. She is no longer in consumer mode. She wants to give to the poor. I give her a coin, which she takes to the guy in the wheelchair. A woman is beside him, maybe his wife. When Lilia gives him the money, they gesture to an array of ashtrays made out of recycled cans. Lilia chooses one, although she doesn't smoke, and doesn't know anyone who does.

ON THE WAY TO the train station, where we will catch our train back to Paris, we see another man sitting with his back against a building, a cardboard sign at his side. This one isn't selling anything. He looks dejected. Defeated. The sign says, "Out of work. Three kids at home."

Lilia looks at me expectantly. I know that she wants to give him money, that she wants to give every unemployed citizen some euros, but we will run out of money ourselves if we do that. There are so many of them. I shake my head slightly and move on.

Later, back at our hotel, we have a dinner of lentil salad, tossed greens, cheese and bread. "What was the most interesting thing about today?" I ask her.

"The train," she says. "It was my first time."

I'm a bit surprised that Joan of Arc (!) didn't have more of an impact. Or that she wasn't more impressed by the Nutella crepes (a specialty of Normandy!), but the train *was* nice, observing the countryside from our plush purple seats *was* very peaceful.

I remind her that we took a train to Versailles, but yes, it *was* different.

Then Lilia becomes pensive. "There were a lot of people without money," she signs.

I nod. I explain that in France, people who are unemployed can go to museums for free. The French understand that art is important and everyone—those with disabilities, children, the poor—is allowed access to the *Mona Lisa*. "Isn't that great?"

I tell her that it was nice of her to give the guy in the wheelchair money, but that he didn't want to beg. It enables him to hang on to a shred of his dignity if he can sell something. Lilia nods thoughtfully.

"I want to come back in the future and help the poor," she says.

Although as her mother I frequently worry that she will end up like that guy in the wheelchair selling homemade ashtrays, that she will have to live in a group home and sort screws for a menial wage, I am heartened by her ambition.

Outside, the lights of the Eiffel Tower sparkle like thousands of gold coins tossed against the night sky.

The Blushing Maiden

By Wednesday morning, Lilia has had enough of sightseeing. She just wants to hang out, connect with her social network in Japan, and draw.

"But this is our last free day!" I tell her. The following afternoon, we will be joining children's book writers and illustrators for a three-day conference. Although we will see some sights during a scheduled Sketch Crawl, this is our last chance to visit the Orsay Museum, one of the places I've always wanted to see but never quite gotten around to on my previous trips to Paris. Although I realize I'm behaving like a Japanese tour guide, trying to cram as many sights and experiences into as little time as possible, I'd really been looking forward to the Orsay.

"We'll just go to *one* museum," I promise. "Tomorrow we'll stay in our room till noon. And the day after, you can play games and read manga on the tablet all you like!" I'll be busy attending workshops and schmoozing with fellow writers, so that will work out just fine. *But not today!*

I open the guidebook and show her pictures of some of the famous paintings on display. "Look! There's the portrait of Van Gogh! You saw the *fake* one already, at the Otsuka Museum in Naruto, but this is the *real* one."

She sighs.

"C'mon! You can just sit in your wheelchair. *I'll push you all the way!*"

Finally, she gives in.

I've sussed out the location, and it looks like it's about a thirty-minute walk from our hotel. It's sunny, the perfect day for a stroll.

On the way, we pass a crime scene. Sirens scream "pi-po pi-po." The police are putting a tape barricade around a café. Bystanders and a truck from the TV station Canal + gather on the opposite corner. Although I'm curious, I'm not quite ready for a heavy dose of reality. I don't want to know what bad thing happened there. I want to stay in my Paris fantasy vacation bubble. The news about the protest was bad enough. Maybe I'll take a look at the newspaper later. More reality: farther up the sidewalk, we pass a homeless guy sprawled on the concrete, surrounded by his stuff.

Lilia seems concerned. "Is he dead?"

"No," I assure her. "He's just sleeping."

OUTSIDE THE Orsay there are sculptures of animals—a bull, an elephant, a rhinoceros. There are also hordes of visitors - tour groups from abroad, along with students on school excursions. I'm not sure where the accessible entrance is, but I see some other people in wheelchairs looking for a way to get in. There's a white French man pushing his companion, a beautiful brown woman with cornrows, who is smoking a cigarette. I follow them. Finally, the guard inside slows the revolving door so that the wheelchair users who have queued up outside can enter.

We follow arrows to elevators, and go down secret passages. There's no one around to direct us. When we finally get inside the crowded galleries, Lilia becomes grumpy because she's not allowed to take photos. I point out the Degas ballerinas, the painting that appears on my Monet shoe box, and another painting by Claude Monet of the Rouen Cathedral, which we saw the day before. She's only mildly interested. She perks up, however, when we come across a woman at an easel, painting her version of a Renoir landscape. We stand for a few minutes watching her mix paint on her palette, and dab colors on the canvas.

She also likes the rooms displaying decorative arts: the plates painted by Rousseau with Japanese carp, another plate with a crab in the path of a Hiroshige-esque wave, the bamboo chairs with enamel seats. And the Salle des Fetes, a wide open ballroom with gorgeous chandeliers and a painted ceiling evokes a "Waaaah!" from Lilia.

From a second floor window we can see the white dome of Sacre Coeur (which is inaccessible via wheelchair—all those steps!) and the bateau mouche chugging along the Seine.

"How about lunch?" I propose.

Like the Louvre, the Orsay Museum consists of many levels, and many elevators, each going to a specific location. It takes a while to figure out how to get to the restaurant, but when we finally do, we are immediately whisked to a table. Next to us is a lone young Japanese woman, digging into a plate of steak and potatoes, several cameras and phones arrayed on the table before her.

The dining room is beautiful, all gilt and chandeliers. A peacock is painted above us, and huge arched windows admit golden light. Bottles of wine are chilling on ice at the center of the room. The staff wears white shirts and black aprons.

We put in our order for peach nectar and the *plat du jour*. While we're waiting for our food to arrive, I ask Lilia, "Why have you been so grumpy?"

"It's embarrassing," she signs. "All those naked bodies."

Ah, the nudes. I didn't realize she found them so disturbing. There are nude sculptures all over the town where we live: in front of the public library, at the corner of the town hall's parking lot, inside lobbies. They're by a renowned local sculptor, my first crush in Japan (he was the art teacher at the school I was assigned to when I first arrived). She's never seemed embarrassed by these bathing women, but then again, she is now at the age when girls become self-conscious.

I promise her a polar bear after lunch. According to the brochure I picked up, the child-friendly sculpture *Ours Blanc* by Francois Pompon is somewhere in this building. Lilia will be able to admire it without blushing. Lunch is fish in cream sauce, accompanied by noodles flavored with lemongrass. With our big dinner at the Eiffel Tower this evening, I'm thinking that we should have just had a little snack. But it's too late now. The food is there before us, then in our stomachs. We have *îles flottantes* - "floating islands" - for dessert.

Lilia is in a better mood after lunch. I'm careful to steer her away from the nudes as we venture in search of the polar bear, or the works of Van Gogh. We never do quite make it to the big white bear, but after asking directions a few times, we manage to locate the correct elevator for the Van Gogh exhibit. A deserted corridor leads to a door that opens onto the gallery. We take a look at the portrait of Vincent van Gogh in blue - the real one, as opposed to the replica we saw before in Naruto. We check out the painting which appears on my Monet shoe box, and then I suggest that we go back to our hotel to rest up for the evening ahead.

Dinner at La Tour Eiffel

DINNER AT THE EIFFEL TOWER on Saturday night would have been the perfect finale for our trip, but over the next three days we'll be participating in a conference for children's book writers and illustrators, and who knows? Maybe we'll want to make dinner plans with the people we meet. So I made reservations at le Jules Verne for Wednesday evening. By then, I figured, we'd be over our jet lag, able to stay awake for a multicourse meal that began at 7PM. We had to go at night so that we would be able to see the city lights sparkling down below. When I made our reservations, I indicated *en francais* that my daughter is a wheelchair user and that we would be needing assistance.

Back at our hotel room, I take a shower and help Lilia into her tights. She puts on her dress, and the new shoes with the leather blossoms on the ankle straps. I shimmy into my gold sequined dress and leopard-print heels. We take photos of each other.

The Eiffel Tower is only fifteen or twenty minutes from our hotel on foot, but as I have learned from experience, we might need a little extra time to flag down a taxi. Plus, I haven't really practiced walking in those four-inch heels, save for one trip from the front door to the mailbox back in Japan. I need to step cautiously. We set out for the taxi stand with half an hour to spare. We haven't even crossed the street before Lilia's left shoe falls off. Dressing up has made her more nervous than usual. Her feet keep tensing up. The other shoe is hanging on by the ankle strap.

Lucky us, there is a guy sitting in his cab, eating fast food. After crumpling the wrapper and brushing his hands together, he gets out to help us.

"Her shoe..." he says.

"I know." I pick it up from the ground and help Lilia into the taxi. Already, she has a run in her tights.

The driver heaves the collapsed wheelchair into the trunk.

"*A la Tour Eiffel!*" I say, working Lilia's foot back into the shoe.

He lets us off near the carousel. I expect that someone will be waiting there, ready to help us. *I'd specifically mentioned the wheelchair when making my reservation.* And since this dinner is going to cost more than our family's monthly food budget, I don't think a little assistance is too much to ask. But there is no one waiting for us.

Hunched over because of the extra height, I push the wheelchair around to the entrance and find a few of our fellow diners. They're assembled at the steps leading to le Jules Verne. To my dismay, some of them are dressed casually. I have already decided that the shoes—both mine and Lilia's—were a bad idea. Why hadn't I let her wear her braces? Who cares if scuffed orange clashes with purple?!

Finally, a restaurant worker appears. We will be taking a private elevator to the second level of the tower. To get to the elevator, we have to go up those stairs. I ease Lilia's foot back into her shoe and, struggling a bit in my four-inch heels, hold her hand as she steps up the stairs. A restaurant employee helps me carry the wheelchair to the first landing.

"Her shoe..." he says.

"Yes, I know." I pick it up. As I crouch beside Lilia, putting the shoe back onto her foot, I hope that I'm not flashing anyone. The gold sequined dress stops at my thighs; it's not made for squatting. Sweat beads at my hairline.

Inside, there is a small dark vestibule, with a steampunk feel: all grinding gears and period posters.

Lilia's shoes fall off again. I give up and carry them in my hand.

We line up to take the elevator in small groups. More stairs lead to the elevator, but this time two men carry Lilia, wheelchair and all, up to the top. I feel a flash of guilt. We shouldn't have come. This place is clearly inaccessible, and now we are inopportuning these men in white shirts and black bow ties. We're being burdensome. And once inside, what if Lilia accidentally spills something, as she sometimes does at home? What if she breaks a dish? Or exclaims loudly? But then I quickly shove these thoughts aside. Lilia has just as much of a right to enjoy a meal in a nice restaurant as the next person. Just as much right as that teen tourist *in casual clothes*, who is also waiting with her family to board the elevator. I recall how a friend in Tokyo who worked with people with disabilities said that the transportation system had become accessible only after officials realized how inconvenient the subway was for wheelchair users. If people like us don't go out and show others how hard it is to get around, *if we don't make ourselves a burden*, they will continue in oblivion. They'll be able to ignore the inaccessibility of their restaurant. We have to do this for wheelchair users everywhere.

As we rise, we can see the snaking Seine, the sky, and the city splayed below. Lilia aims my camera down, snapping photos of the metal struts.

The elevator door opens to a battalion of waiters bustling about. We're shown to our table, which is not, alas, next to the window, but we can still glimpse the city beyond. I slide my feet out of the leopard-print heels - ahh! - and line up my shoes and Lilia's under the table.

The restaurant interior has a sci-fi feel with its white domed plates reminding me of UFOs, and the mosaic on the ceiling resembling a moonscape, or the aftermath of a volcanic eruption.

"What is that?" I ask the sommelier as he pours my champagne.

"The plates represent the base of the Eiffel Tower, as if you are looking from above."

"And the ceiling?"

"It's a map of Paris."

Our waiter, a blond *mec* with a sardonic smile, appears. *"En français ou anglais?"*

"En français." Why not? I spent many years studying French. I need to put it to some use. Plus, speaking French makes me feel sophisticated. And Lilia is so impressed.

The waiter offers to take our photo. When he gives the camera back to Lilia, she takes a picture of the butter, then the cheese puffs and my glass of champagne, then the starter, something made with lentils and wasabi.

I try to explain the significance of Jules Verne to Lilia. Admittedly, we have concentrated more on female figures in French history while preparing for our trip. But she's watched the Jackie Chan version of *Around the World in 80 Days*, and she's been on the "Journey to the Center of the Earth Ride" at Tokyo Disneyland, so I figure she has some idea.

EVENING BEGINS to fall on Paris, and soon streetlights illuminate the avenues below. Car headlights flash and flicker. Even the river, reflecting lights from its banks, seems to be strewn with stars. I consider tottering over on my heels to the window to take a photo, but I am pleasantly buzzed from the champagne. I don't really want to move.

The waiter brings our next course, settling the plates in front of us with a flourish.

Lilia grabs my phone and takes a photo of the asparagus in sabayon, which is fat and juicy, and from Provence.

I confess I was worried that the waiters and other diners would look askance at a child in a wheelchair, but the staff seems charmed. When the bread basket comes around for the second and third time, and Lilia indicates that she wants more, I frown. But the waiter, calling her "*la petite*," and "*Mademoiselle*," encourages Lilia to help herself. We are in Paris—why not? City of Lights! City of Bread!

During the meat course, the Eiffel Tower begins to sparkle, like the champagne in my glass, like the sequins on my dress. Everything seems so perfect in this moment.

"Ever since you were born, I've been dreaming of bringing you to Paris," I tell Lilia. Even before I became a mother, I'd imagined a mother-daughter trip just like this one. The idea first popped into my head when one of my adult English students in Japan told me that she was taking her teenaged daughter to Vienna. Lilia's eyes widen, and she leans toward me. "Really?" She loves hearing stories about her babyhood. She loves knowing that we've had the same dream of Paris.

"Yes. When I learned that you couldn't walk, I wasn't sure if it was possible. But here we are!"

Moved, she wipes away a tear with her knuckle. "Thank you!"

The next course is the fish course: halibut in a frothy green sauce evocative of matcha. One blade of lemongrass is artfully arranged on top of it. Lilia takes another picture. I take another bite, savoring the subtle flavors.

By the time we've finished the meat course, and two of three dessert courses (pistachio ice cream), three hours have passed and the lights on the tower have flickered two more times. Stuffed to the gills, we are unable to finish the homemade marshmallows. Unbelievably, we leave chocolate on the table. I read somewhere that the French don't do doggy bags, but our waiter kindly offers to wrap up the remaining sweets for us to take back to our hotel.

When we are ready to go, I put my shoes back on and ask the hostess to call a taxi for us. As we shrug into our coats, she hands Lilia a couple of packages of madeleines, and chats with me.

"Doesn't she speak?" she asks.

"No," I say. "She's deaf."

We talk a little about the differences between American and Japanese and French Sign Language. "Thank you" in ASL is about the same as "Bonjour" in French Sign Language, I've discovered.

"It must be hard to get around," she says, referring to the wheelchair.

"It was easier than I'd imagined," I say. Although Paris is not altogether accessible, we've managed to cover quite a bit of ground. I'm feeling proud of myself, and of Lilia.

"Is it just the two of you?" the hostess asks with a touch of pity.

I'm not sure if she's referring to the evening, or to our lives in general. Maybe she imagines that I'm a single mom, struggling to raise my handicapped child alone. I don't want her to think of us in that way.

"We've come alone, but my husband and son are home. In Japan," I say. "It was my daughter's dream to come to Paris."

"And here you are."

"Yes, here we are."

"*Bon courage*," she says, when the elevator arrives. "Good luck!"

Lilia waves enthusiastically with one hand, gripping the bag of madeleines in the other, while I feel curiously deflated. Although my daughter's disabilities are, at first glance, the most remarkable thing about her—about us—why do we always have to talk about them? I don't go around feeling sorry for myself, and I don't want other people to pity me, or Lilia. I want them to see Lilia, not as a deaf girl in a wheelchair, not as my inescapable burden, but as a well-rounded individual with a place in the world. She has a rich interior life. She has ideas and opinions. She is aware of things. If only Lilia could communicate directly with people who she meets, they would understand just how interesting and informed she is. Forget about the wheelchair. She'd rather talk about UFOs and Marie

Antoinette, manga and murder mysteries and the possible existence of fairies. Also, she is a font of information.

I want the taciturn elevator operator to understand this, too, which is why I blurt, "My daughter told me that there have been many suicides from the Eiffel Tower."

He makes some vague noise. Obviously, this is not suitable elevator conversation. My husband often says that I am incapable of "reading the air," and maybe he is right. Even so, I imagine that Yoshi, who'd asked Tokyo Disneyland employees about the Day of the Earthquake, would have asked the same thing.

"But she said that precautions have been taken," I babble on, "and that there aren't so many anymore."

"*Eh, voila*," he replies.

Among Illustrators

I'VE BEEN A MEMBER of the Society of Children's Book Writers and Illustrators for several years, and I'm about to publish my first young adult novel which is set in Paris. When I discovered that that European chapters of SCBWI were holding their first ever Europolitan Conference at the end of March, I signed up.

"Can I bring my daughter along?" I asked.

"Sure," the organizers responded.

"Just so you know, she uses a wheelchair..."

The building isn't accessible, but I figured that if Lilia can make it up the three flights of stairs at her school, she can probably handle the stairs at the Paris College of Art. If not, the organizers suggested she could hang out on the first floor.

I'd figured that after a week of sightseeing and togetherness, Lilia would be ready to stay put with a sketchbook or games on my tablet. Also, I was sure she would be reinvigorated by meeting new people. I was right. Lilia is excited when I tell her about the Sketch Crawl scheduled for Thursday afternoon.

The idea is that writers and illustrators will gather and visit sites related to Charlotte Corday and take notes or make quick drawings along the way. Our guide will be an expat writer who's turned a story into an award-winning app.

We're supposed to meet at Le Palais Royal. Lilia and I take a taxi. The driver drops us off in front of a square where an artist has drawn a huge picture in chalk. I'm immediately accosted by a deaf Rom woman, who waves a clipboard in my face. She motions for me to write my name and address. I'm amazed to meet a deaf woman on the street like this, and at first I feel that there is some sort of connection between Lilia, this woman and me. By the time I finish writing my contact details, I realize I've been suckered into a beggar's ruse. She indicates that I'm to write the amount of my donation. Huh? I write "1 Euro," because that's about all I can spare. Our cash supply is rapidly dwindling, and we still have a couple of taxi rides and dinners to pay for. The woman holds up two fingers. I shake my head, hand over a coin, and hustle Lilia away from the crowd.

Snow has begun to fall. I look around for our group, and finally find a bunch of women in parkas and hats and a couple of men with notebooks gathered in front of a fountain. We are immediately welcomed. Kristen, an American illustrator living in Germany, tells me that her husband had lived in Japan, and that she has an uncle with cerebral palsy. Upon learning that Lilia has a cochlear implant, Sabrina, an illustrator from Belgium, confides that she is partially deaf in one ear. She quickly wins Lilia over by promising to bring her chocolate the following day and offers to push her wheelchair.

Once everyone has assembled, Sarah, our guide, starts telling us the story of Charlotte Corday, a poor young woman who'd left home, and come to Paris to assassinate Jean Marat.

The snow has turned into sleet. We move into a nearby covered arcade to sketch and take notes. Lilia and I are stationed in front of a shop window full of Chanel bags. Passersby slow and glance at our sketches. A French woman pauses to praise Lilia's drawing of the fountain. And then a thin, older woman comes out of the shop.

"Could you take this...whatever you're doing and do it

someplace else?" she says in a disdainful tone. "I think that would be better."

For a moment, I wonder if she thinks that I have brought my daughter here to sketch for coins. Maybe she thinks we are beggars, huddled against the wall, waiting to prey upon her wealthy customers. I'm not in the mood for a scene, however, so I apologize and we move away.

Our next stop is the site of a printing press which was in operation during the French Revolution, followed by a visit to the shop where Corday bought the knife she used to kill Marat while he took a bath. Nearby, a group of men play petanque, flinging silver balls in the sandy alley. Lilia whips out her pencil and draws the game. And then Sabrina and Lilia sketch each other.

To warm up, we stop at the Starbucks near the Louvre. I spot a group of people in the café conversing in Sign Language. I recall that the world's first school for the deaf was established in Paris in 1760 by Abbé Charles-Michel de l'Épée. I'm disappointed that we haven't had a chance to meet with Lilia's hearing-impaired peers, but she seems to be getting along just fine with the hearing, English-speaking adults we are with, in spite of a lack of a common language. Pictures are a means of communication, I realize, as effective as any tongue.

On the Pont des Arts, we come across joggers, dog-walkers and lovers. The bridge is famous for the padlocks that couples attach to the chain link fence proclaiming everlasting devotion: Marc and Sinead, Mike and Stephen, Keio and Shiho, Kyle Heart Sophie. "Together in Paris—Marry Me?" A swath of late afternoon sunlight falls on the Seine. Along the banks are the spindly branches of trees, not yet in bud.

At the end of the Scrawl Crawl, we cram ourselves into a small restaurant specializing in Basque cuisine. The only bathroom on the premises is down a narrow, winding staircase. Luckily, Lilia doesn't have to go.

THE CONFERENCE is held in the Paris branch of the Parson's

School of Design, just around the corner from our hotel. Students mill about with their cigarettes and portfolios. I hear English everywhere. The blue-doored building is old, and there's no elevator, no Wi-Fi. We arrive a little early to get Lilia up the stairs. Gary, an American illustrator living in Sweden, helps to carry the wheelchair up to the second floor studio where the first session will be held.

We settle on paint-splattered stools amidst canvases featuring abstract art a la Jasper Johns. The room fills with children's book writers, illustrators, editors and agents from the Netherlands, Dubai, Germany, Israel, France and Britain, among other places. I worry that Lilia will quickly become bored and demand attention, or at least request a translation of the proceedings, but she manages to content herself with drawing and reading and playing games on my tablet for the next two hours.

At lunchtime, Sabrina brings her some Belgian chocolate, as promised. Mina, from the Netherlands, gives her a little booklet of writing prompts. Kristen, who's told Lilia that one of her hobbies is drawing underwater, gives Lilia a notebook as thanks for helping to arrange the snacks when we'd first arrived. Throughout the day, professional illustrators praise her drawings. Lilia has found her tribe.

As she becomes more comfortable, we split up. Lilia is allowed to sit in on the presentations for illustrators, and I attend the ones for writers. Later, during the post-conference cocktail party, Lilia drinks apple juice and wheels around freely, taking in the illustrators' exhibition, while I chat with an expat writer who'd lived in South Korea. I also meet a Taiwanese-born illustrator who's working on a picture book about robots, and a kilt-wearing former sea captain who's writing a fantasy series for mid-grade readers. Lilia fills her sketchbook with portraits of the people she meets. At dinner, with me as her translator, she quizzes our companions: "What animal don't you like? What food do you like?" and everyone answers patiently.

When we finally part ways for good, I discover that she has met people that I hadn't spoken to at all. Everyone seems to know her name. The American illustrator who lives in Sweden gives her a kiss on the cheek.

WE HAVE OUR LAST breakfast of the trip in the hotel's dining room. This time, I remember to cook our eggs.

Lilia starts telling me a story about Hanako—not the Japanese woman sculpted by Auguste Rodin, but a Japanese ghost who supposedly haunts toilets. I realize that, as we prepare for our departure, her thoughts are veering toward Japan, toward home.

"How was Paris?" I ask.

"It was fun," she replies, "but we didn't get to go to the place where Marie Antoinette was held prisoner." Lilia has read in the guidebook that a lock of Marie's hair is on display, and she wanted to see it. The Conciergerie had been on the agenda for the Scrawl Crawl, but we'd run out of time and didn't make it there.

"It's okay," she adds. "Next time...."

Personally, I'm a little disappointed that we didn't get to visit Monet's former home in Giverny. It's closed to visitors in March.

In the taxi on the way to the airport for our flight home, I listen to the radio. The announcer says that the previous evening, around the time that we would have been having our meat course, someone called in a bomb threat to the Eiffel Tower. Over a thousand people were evacuated from the area. My mind flashes to an image of Lilia in her wheelchair and me, teetering on four-inch leopard-print heels, trying to cram ourselves into the elevator like Titanic passengers rushing for the lifeboats. I clear my head and sink back into the car seat, flooded with relief. All things considered, our trip has been a success.

I don't tell Lilia what I've heard on the radio. She doesn't need to know. As the Eiffel Tower, the Tomb of Napoleon, the

Monoprix, the Louvre Museum, the Champs-Élysées and all of Paris recedes behind us, Lilia signs, "I want to come back!"

That's my girl.

In the months to come, I will discover that our French excursion was everything that I had hoped it would be for her. She'll impress her teachers and classmates with her new knowledge of French customs and culture. Using the photos that we took for reference, she will paint images of the Eiffel Tower, the Mona Lisa, and other things. Her paintings will be published in a magazine for children. Now that she has a wider view of the world, she will be more attentive to current events. Whenever we catch a glimpse of France on TV, we will put our hands over our hearts and squeal in unison. No matter what happens in the future, we'll always have Paris.

One More Monet

TWO YEARS AFTER our epic trip to Paris, Lilia graduates from the brand new junior high school. Construction of the School for the Deaf and Blind, complete with elevator and accessible toilets on every floor, was finished a year ahead of schedule. No longer all alone, Lilia was in the same class as another boy, up on the third floor. She passed Level 8 of the Japanese kanji proficiency test (with flying colors), which puts her at about a fourth-grade reading level. Thanks to her frequent texting to friends, her written Japanese has also improved. In a month, Lilia will begin high school in the same building. To celebrate this milestone, she and I are taking another mother-daughter trip—this time, just overnight—to Naoshima, an island off the coast of Shikoku.

Once known mainly as a site for dumping industrial waste, Naoshima has been revitalized through a series of art projects. I made a reservation for us at the Benesse House Museum, in which each of the ten rooms has original artwork and a view of the Seto Inland Sea.

I invite Jio along, but he declines. The week before our departure, he takes the entrance exam for his first-choice high school, which happens to be the one at which his father worked when he was born. The school is one of the most competitive in the prefecture and he has studied long and hard. To celebrate the completion of the exam, come what may, he is having a couple of classmates sleep over. Yoshi will be there to make sure things don't get out of hand.

I've been planning for us to go by bus-taxi-ferry and to be met by the hotel shuttle bus. This way, Lilia and I will be able to chat in sign language en route, and I'll be able to read and relax. However, a light drizzle is predicted for the day of our trip and dealing with a wheelchair in the rain is never fun. I decide to go by car.

ON THE MORNING of our departure, Yoshi makes a bento for us: hand-packed rice balls and sautéed pork and vegetables. I load the suitcase decorated with hot air balloons and Lilia's wheelchair into the car and we set out for Takamatsu, an hour's drive north. For most of the way, we're on the highway flying past the lushly forested hills of Shikoku, past signs warning of wandering wild boars, through mountain tunnels. Once in the city, I follow the directions given by the navigation system on my iPhone and manage to get us to the ferry terminal and onto the boat. Most of the other vehicles are dump trucks, perhaps loaded with industrial waste for dumping in the northwest part of the island. Because there is no easy way to get Lilia up on deck, we stay in the car, in the belly of the boat, only vaguely aware of our progress across the sea.

"Go look," Lilia encourages.

I get out of the car and peek out the window. All I can see is water.

We disembark about an hour later at Miyanoura Port. Along with the fishing boats bobbing gently in the harbor, we see the enormous red polka-dotted pumpkin created by Yayoi Kusama in a park to the left of the Visitor's Center. Signs helpfully indicate directions to the 007 Museum (a room full of kitschy James Bond memorabilia which I'd visited once before) and the various art museums. In addition to the Benesse House Art Site, there is a museum devoted to the works of Korean artist Lee Ufan (whose work was recently the subject of a major exhibition at Versailles), the Chichu Art Museum, and the Art House Project, a group of abandoned houses in which contemporary art is now exhibited.

I inadvertently take the scenic route down narrow neighborhood streets, winding up mountain roads which drop off to the sea. Wisps of fog hover over the cove, backed by cliffs, reminding me of Chinese ink paintings. Luckily, there is no traffic to speak of, only a few random hikers and cyclists. No one honks at my slow, careful driving. I can hear Lilia snapping photos of the spectacular view in the backseat. The road descends, and I spot the campsite with rows of white yurts off to our left. A guardhouse is stationed in front of the road that leads to the Art Site on the right. He verifies that we are indeed guests at the hotel and directs us the rest of the way.

In addition to the museum, the Art Site includes a grassy area featuring colorful child-friendly sculptures by internationally celebrated artists such as Karel Appel, Niki de Saint Phalle, and Dan Graham. Another Yayoi Kusama pumpkin, this one yellow, is located further down the beach. We drive past the Terrace Restaurant where we will dine later this evening, and *Drink a Cup of Tea*, a sculpture of a blue tea cup by Kazuo Katase, which is balanced on a stone wall, and then we begin to climb again. I catch a glimpse of an overturned yellow boat on another beach in a far cove.

We finally arrive at the Benesse House Museum, a modern concrete grey structure also designed by Ando. I unload Lilia's wheelchair, help her out of the car, and push her up the ramp to the entrance.

"Welcome!" The young woman at the reception desk is French. I'd been prepared to speak Japanese, so it takes me a moment to adjust. I find out later that forty percent of visitors to the island are from abroad, so it makes perfect sense to have an international multilingual staff.

The receptionist hands over our room key, which is attached to a piece of driftwood in keeping with the natural surroundings, and we follow a young Japanese woman onto the elevator. We get off on the third floor and go down a hushed, dim corridor to our room. Children are not allowed to stay in the museum hotel, presumably because the rooms contain valuable artwork, but also perhaps because they are noisy. This ban on children somehow goes against the "art is for everyone" philosophy espoused by the French and, supposedly, the Benesse founder Fukutake himself. I guess the children, as yet in a wild state, are meant to stay in the yurts on the beach. The website also makes it quite clear that there will be no discounts for individuals with special needs. The hotel does not have "barrier-free" accommodations, but I figure we'll manage.

"Waaah!" Lilia exclaims, as she wheels herself into the room. The furnishings are in blonde wood, and the twin beds are covered with bright white duvets. The art is *Stern* by Thomas Ruff, paintings of a star-studded night sky. I'd actually tried to reserve one of two rooms featuring paintings by German artist Imi Knoebel of Grace Kelly, whom Lilia would have recognized from TV and her manga biography, but the rooms were booked throughout the month. Nevertheless, Lilia is completely satisfied, especially since she doesn't even need a password to access the hotel's Wi-Fi network. She immediately begins texting her friends.

I sigh. "Let's go check out the art."

The door is too heavy for her to open by herself. I wouldn't want to leave her alone in this room, even if she'd rather stay here texting her friends. She takes a recharger out of her backpack and connects it to her iPad, then follows me into the corridor, albeit a tad reluctantly.

Much of the art in the museum was inspired by Naoshima and created on-site. Richard Long's walks around the island in 1997 were the impetus for his four works in the first gallery we enter. *Inland Sea Driftwood Circle* is just that: a circle composed of wood laid out on the floor. As far as I can tell, nothing fixes it in place. I keep an eye on Lilia's wheelchair, making sure that she doesn't accidentally back into the installation, knocking something out of place. I can't help wondering if the museum staff sometimes has to fix the composition. This is a land of earthquakes, after all. And don't they have to dust the wood from time to time?

Another circle of stones—*Full Moon Stone Circle*—is outside, and two other large circles painted in earthy tones, *River Avon Mud Circles*, dominate a white wall.

"What does this one look like to you?" I ask Lilia, gesturing at the wall.

She studies it for a moment. "Doughnuts."

We take in Yukinori Yanagi's *Banzai Corner*, in which hundreds of Ultraman dolls with their hands raised are lined up in front of a mirror; there is a swimming pool by David Hockney, and Jasper Johns's *White Alphabets*, which Lilia finds underwhelming.

"They're famous artists." I tell her that Jasper Johns studied art at my alma mater, the University of South Carolina.

She leans in for a closer look. Yayoi Kusama aside, she hasn't had much exposure to modern art until now. Maybe this trip will open her mind to possibilities.

"You could probably create something like this." I point at Cy Twombly's *Untitled I*, which is composed of repeated squiggles.

She nods. "Yes, I could."

A long ramp leads to the first floor of the museum where Jonathan Borofsky's *Three Chattering Men* nod their heads and say, "Chatter chatter chatter chatter chatter." There is also an installation by American Jennifer Bartlett of overturned yellow and black rowboats. A painting of the boats — *Yellow and Black Boats* — hangs on the wall just above. I recognize the boats that I saw earlier down on the beach.

In another room, we find another site-specific work created by Jannis Kounellis. He has rolled up driftwood, old kimonos, Japanese paper, and earthenware in lead plates. The installation is untitled, leaving it open to interpretation. I see the shape of logs and a connection to industry in the materials used, an echo of Naoshima's past. "What does this one look like to you?" I ask Lilia.

"Flowers," she signs. "Roses."

Okay, I can see that, too.

Although the galleries are, for the most part, accessible, one requires steps. I take a look and report back to Lilia. "It's like white paper."

She doesn't feel compelled to see for herself.

Lilia, as anyone might be able to ascertain from her bright pink sweater and orange leg braces, loves color. Therefore, it's no surprise that her favorite painting of the day is David Hockney's *A Walk Around the Courtyard Acatlan,* done in the vivid pinks and oranges of Mexico.

"I want to paint something like that," she signs. "Something big."

UPON CHECKING IN, I was handed a card entitling me to a free glass of sparkling wine in the Museum Café at 4:30PM. After going through the museum, we still have some time until Happy Hour, and the other attractions are not open today, so I propose a visit to the park further down the hill.

I park the car behind the shop and restaurants and we take a little stroll down the hill. Crows caw and pigeons rustle in the underbrush. Several foreigners cruise by on rented bicycles. Japanese tourists seem to be in the minority. We pose for photos in front of some of the sculptures, including the yellow pumpkin, until Lilia says that she is cold and wants to go back to the hotel.

When 4:30 rolls around, Lilia is once again engrossed in her iPad.

"Shall we go have a drink? Some juice?"

"You go ahead," she signs. "I'll wait here."

I picture myself sitting all alone with my glass of sparkling wine while couples chat and laugh at the surrounding tables. How sad. "No way. This is our mother-daughter trip. We're supposed to spend time together talking." Sure, we could hang out in our room until dinner, but this hotel isn't cheap, and I want to take advantage of all of the freebies we've been offered. We are no longer poor since I have a full-time job for the first time since the twins' birth, but I haven't quite forgotten what it was like to be broke.

She sighs.

"Look, you can bring your iPad with you." No doubt she'll have access to Wi-Fi in the café.

We take the elevator down one floor and are shown to a table with a view of the sea. The sun is slowly sinking.

An elderly gentleman and the Japanese woman we met earlier are tending the bar. "Would you like sparkling wine, or a mimosa?" the man asks. "A mimosa is a mix of sparkling wine and orange juice."

"I'll have a glass of wine," I say, although he seems most enthusiastic about the mixed drink, "and orange juice for my daughter."

The white-haired gentleman deposits our beverages in front of us and shows me a photo of the sunset on his smart phone.

"Do you take a photo every day?" I ask him.

"Yes," he says. "Today the sun will set at 6:20PM."

I ask if he was born here on Naoshima.

"Yes." But like most young people, he left the island after finishing school. Back in the day, there were a hundred kids in his elementary school class. Now there are about twenty. Naoshima has a junior high school, but local kids have to go to Takamatsu for high school. "I lived in Yokohama for forty years, and then I came back," he says.

The Japanese woman tells me that she is originally from Kyoto.

"Does your daughter like art?" she asks.

"Yes." I try to get Lilia to show the young woman some of the manga-style drawings that she has done on her iPad, but she shakes her head. I explain to the woman that we live in

Tokushima, and that Lilia and I went to Paris a couple of years ago, where we visited many museums.

"One of my coworkers, the one you met when you checked in, is French," she confirms. "She just went to Paris. Naoshima is very popular among French people."

I glance around the café. The other tables are mostly occupied by Westerners. From their accents, I'm guessing they're Americans and Germans. There is one Japanese couple.

By now my "one free drink" is gone, but the white-haired gentleman brings me a mimosa, unbidden, and Lilia another orange juice. *O.mo.te.na.shi.* Talk about Japanese hospitality.

"Thank you!"

Later, we freshen up and change our clothes. Lilia debuts a dark purple chiffon dress, and adorns her wrist with her Eiffel Tower charm bracelet. I'd brought along her "Paris shoes," the subdued grey ones that kept falling off, but after viewing the brightly painted sculptures in the park, I'm thinking Lilia's orange leg braces are so "Niki de Saint Phalle." And me? I go for a slinky sleeveless black dress paired with a duster patterned with silver tendrils, and huge pearlescent beads. My shoes, of course, are from Monet, the ones I wore to the Japanese Culture Center in Paris.

After the drinks, I'm glad there's a hotel shuttle to the seaside French restaurant. I wouldn't be able to manage the twisty drive in the dark. The van lets us out at the back entrance of the Benesse House Park Building. A woman leads Lilia and me to an elevator, reaches inside and pushes a button. We get off on the first floor, finding ourselves in a dark, empty corridor. The receptionist gave me a map and showed me how to get to the restaurant, but that was three hours and two glasses of sparkling wine ago. I forgot to bring the map. Now I'm a tad confused, and I'm starting to wonder if this will be the Japanese Culture Center in Paris all over again. I open one door, which leads to a lounge. Nope, not here. Then I push through the door that takes us outside and reorient myself. We go down a hallway past the spa, past the gift shop, and arrive at the Umi no Hoshi (Stars of the Sea) restaurant in time for our 6PM reservation.

A friendly Japanese waiter seats us at a table next to a window which looks out onto the sea through the black pines.

"Naoshima is great," Lilia signs. "I can't decide if I like Paris or Naoshima better."

I laugh. Lilia's enduring enthusiasm for new places is what makers her such a great travel companion. Paris and Naoshima are vastly different. Maybe she would get bored after a few days on this small island, but it's beautiful here, with the lush vegetation, the craggy inclines, and the stretch of sea. Plus, there's the art. "It is very nice here," I agree.

The waiter brings our first course, an amuse-bouche consisting of a micro-salad and fish mousse. Lilia takes a photo of the food.

She photographs the bread and the olive oil, pressed from the olives of Shodoshima, another small island nearby. She takes a picture of the fish. Lilia's piece has been thoughtfully cut into bite-sized pieces. When I point this out to her, she is visibly moved.

The waiter comes by with the bread basket and Lilia takes another piece.

"Will the meat be tough?" she asks, thinking of the next course.

I realize that she is worried about using the silverware to cut her own beef. Although she has had practice cutting meat at home and during school restaurant outings, she finds it a bit of a nuisance. "They'll probably cut that for you, too."

She's glad that people are willing to help her, but she tells me that she is worried about the future. "Is there some work that I can do by myself? Will I always need help?"

In junior high school, she couldn't do an internship at the bakery because of her wheelchair. To maneuver around, she would have to touch the chair, which is supposedly dirty, according to the people in charge. When preparing food, hygiene is especially important. I can't help thinking that, with a few adaptions, she would be able to bake bread while maintaining health standards. Nevertheless, her one-day junior high school internship was at one of the Welfare-supported work centers where she completed menial tasks. I'm hoping that she will have the chance to try work that is more interesting and challenging in high school. She says that she wants to do work that is related to art. To me, this seems entirely possible.

"You'll find something that you can do," I tell her. Even if her work isn't directly related to art, she can still create paintings and drawings and sculptures and installations. Maybe we can work on something together someday; I can write the words, and she can produce the illustrations.

By the time our beef arrives, the sun has gone down and the beach beyond is cloaked in total darkness. I can't even see the stars of the sea. As I predicted, the meat has been discreetly cut so Lilia will not have to grapple with the fork and knife. She takes a picture of her plate. Each morsel is tender enough to melt in our mouths.

Dessert is chocolate soup and ice cream for me, and strawberry soup and ice cream for her. It's beautiful and delicious. Lilia takes a photo, and then waits a tad impatiently for me to sip my after-dinner coffee.

The restaurant arranges for a car to take us back to the hotel since the shuttle is no longer running. Back in our hotel room, we change our clothes and Lilia starts to grab for her iPad, but I propose another look at the art. One of the perks of staying in the Museum Hotel is the privilege of visiting the galleries after hours. We have until 11PM.

At night, *The Chattering Men* are silent. The docents are gone. We could touch the art, and no one would know. Lilia could get out of her wheelchair, crawl up the steps, and enter the inaccessible gallery to see the all-white paintings, and no one would notice.

The lighting is different at night. Jennifer Bartlett's yellow and black boats are reflected in the glass window on the opposite wall, and Kan Yasuda's stone sculpture glows dimly in the moonlight. The blinking neon words of Bruce Nauman's *100 Live and Die* are kind of spooky in the dark: "Laugh and Die." "Cry and Live." "Eat and Die." I don't translate the signs for Lilia. I would rather tell her to "Write and Paint." "Eat and Dance." "Sleep and Dream."

IN THE MORNING, our view of the sea is obscured by fog. We learn that the ferries aren't running due to poor visibility. I feel a little nervous about driving on the twisty mountain roads sans guardrails in the fog and hope it will dissipate by the time we've finished our breakfast.

We go down the ramp to the first floor of the museum. The Issen Restaurant is just past the colorful David Hockney painting that Lilia likes. Inside, we are seated near the window. I have a great view of Andy Warhol's *Flowers*.

"I don't think Daddy would like it here," I muse, as I spread apricot jam on my croissant.

"Why not?"

"Well, for one thing, there are no golf courses," I tell her. "Also, Daddy doesn't really like to look at art." When we'd first started dating, we went to some art exhibits at the Prefectural Museum in Tokushima City. Once, he sat down on a bench and fell asleep in the gallery. Granted, he was hungover on that day, but after we were married, he stopped going to art museums with me.

Lilia nods, thoughtfully. "Some people like looking at art, and some people don't."

An older Japanese woman dressed ostentatiously in a flowing red tunic and red leggings comes into the restaurant. She wears a scowl. She ducks her head into the kitchen to make some demand. Later, I see the museum staff fussing around her, and herding her into a private car. I never do find out who she is, but I think she must be from the big city, or maybe she's a famous artist.

After breakfast, I tell the receptionist that we're going to the Chichu Museum. "Could you let them know that we have a wheelchair?"

The receptionist picks up the phone. I settle our bill and we go to the car. Visibility is a bit better now, and I realize that we'd come the day before in a roundabout way. The Chichu Museum, which was also designed by Tadao Ando, and which houses five paintings from Claude Monet's *Water Lily* series, is just down the hill.

Although there is no discount for individuals with disabilities, kids aged fifteen and under are admitted for free, so I'm the only one who needs a ticket. When we arrive, a staff member is waiting to let us in. She lifts the chain blocking the rear entrance and I drive up the hill. A young woman in a white blouse and navy culottes meets us at the top and ushers us inside.

The museum is built into the mountain, like a bunker, and lit by natural lighting. The walls are grey concrete and most of the staff is dressed in what looks like white lab coats. The brochure advises us to "maintain a quiet environment in the museum." It's like a hospital, or a church, but with a sci-fi vibe.

We are mainly here to see the Monet, so we make that our first order of business. We descend an elevator to a dark hall in which there is a rack of slippers.

"Please change your shoes," the docent says.

She has prepared wheel covers for Lilia's wheelchair tires, but they don't seem to fit, so she gets a cloth and thoroughly wipes the tires. Finally, we are ready to enter the hallowed space.

The walls are blindingly white, the better to offset the deep blues and purples of Monet's sun-dappled pond. Unlike in Musée de l'Orangerie, no one is allowed to sketch here. There are no children. No one speaks. Lilia spends several seconds before each panel: *Water Lilies, Cluster of Grass, Water Lilies, Reflection of Weeping Willows, Water Lily Pond.*

The Chichu Museum houses work by only three artists—

four, if you include architect Ando. The second exhibit that we visit is *Open Field* by James Turrell. Although we have only traveled a short way down the hall, the docents wipe Lilia's wheelchair tires again as we wait in line. Only eight people are permitted into the space at a time. While we are waiting, a docent greets Lilia using sign language.

She looks at me and smiles.

I leave my shoes in a different shoe rack and enter in stocking feet. Visitors are invited to walk up a set of stairs to enter a room lit by fluorescent light. For the full effect, one must enter the room but there is no wheelchair ramp. Turrell obviously wasn't thinking about accessibility when he designed this piece, and yet it seems to me that it wouldn't have required much.

Lilia and I look up into the space from the bottom as the others mount the steps with reverence. They look like they are about to enter a spaceship, or maybe on their way to some ritual of worship. They look like cult members.

"Do you want me to help you up the stairs?" I ask Lilia.

"No," she signs. "But you go ahead."

"No, I'll wait here with you."

"Go, go."

"Well, okay." I walk the steps and enter the blue-lit space. It's discomfiting, surreal. A tall Western woman nearby, who seems to be here alone, gasps with joy or admiration or awe. I'm not sure what this all means, but when I go back down the steps and rejoin Lilia, I feel somewhat relieved.

The final exhibit, which also involves stairs, is *Time/Timeless/No Time* by Walter De Maria. Once again, Lilia urges me to go up the stairs. She waits below, regarding the large black sphere at the center of it all, and the wooden sculptures covered with gold leaf which suggest the roman numerals of a clock. Light comes in through a window on the ceiling. On sunny days, the gold must be dazzling.

"Ready for cake?" I ask Lilia, when I've returned to her. It hasn't been that long since breakfast, but I think it would be nice to try the desserts made according to Monet's own recipes, which are sold in the Chichu Café.

Lilia nods.

She pulls up to the long, blond wooden table facing the sea, which is still shrouded in mist. There are some books on hand, including a picture book about Monet, which I grab for Lilia to read while I get our food. I order a madeleine for myself, and vanilla ice cream for Lilia.

"His wife died when she was only thirty," Lilia tells me.

"Oh, yeah?" To tell the truth, I don't know all that much about Monet's personal life. I know that his wife was named Camille, and that she was the subject of several of his most famous paintings, including *La Japonaise*, and that he once received Blondelle Malone, an artist from Columbia, South Carolina, who traveled via Japan to meet him. I know that he had a big bushy beard, and that he had some problems with his eyesight. Lilia quickly uncovers this fact as well.

"He had cataracts," she says, after reading a little further. Now that the School for the Deaf has combined with the School for the Blind, she is especially sensitive to issues related to eyesight.

The nuclear cataracts clouding Monet's vision in both eyes caused his perception of color to change when he was in his mid-sixties, though he wasn't diagnosed until 1912, when he was 72. *The Water Lily* paintings in the Chichu Museum were completed over the years 1914-1926. In a letter to a friend, Monet wrote, "My poor eyesight makes me see everything in a complete fog. It's very beautiful all the same and it's this which I'd love to have been able to convey."

Although the water lilies in his pond at Giverny were a major theme late in his life, earlier paintings depict families eating dinner, an apple tart, a cut of meat, and preserved apricots. Monet, it seems, was something of a gourmand. The madeleine made according to his recipe is certainly tasty and I decide to buy a copy of a Monet recipe book in the gift shop on the way out.

While we are browsing the key rings and notepads and art books, someone knocks into something, creating a loud sound.

I catch the eye of an American guy in the gift shop. "Making noise is forbidden," I mock admonish.

"You're not supposed to breathe," his girlfriend adds.

We exchange smirks, and I can't help wondering what Monet would have made of this place. He'd have had to put out his cigarette and wipe the garden mud from his shoes. He wouldn't have been allowed to speak.

THE FERRIES STILL AREN'T running due to fog. We wander around the port, where bicycles are rented for five hundred yen per day, and walk down back alleys, stumbling upon the I Love Yu (*yu*, being the Japanese word for hot water) bathhouse, a veritable palace of kitsch designed by Shinro Ohtake, whose work appears in the Museum of Modern Art in New York City and the Victoria and Albert Museum in London, among other places. The outside walls are decorated with a hodgepodge of ceramic tiles and variously shaped blocks of wood. A fake penguin stands at the center of a fountain, and a bubble gum dispenser issues badges printed with the artist's name. The sixty-something couple who run the place seem utterly unphased by Lilia's wheelchair. The gentleman helps me heave her, chair and all, up the steps. Lilia crawls into the changing room.

The bottom of the bath itself is inlaid with coins and photos. A large, realistically sculpted elephant looks down on bathers from the top of the wall that separates the men's bath from the women's area. Plants grow in jungly profusion on the other side of a glass wall. Who knew a soak in hot water could be so much fun?

SINCE WE'LL BE missing dinner, I suggest that we eat an early meal before boarding the ferry. Lilia agrees. I'm not too hungry, but we duck into a mom-and-pop place across from the ferry terminal which advertises, in magic marker on a white board, flounder in all its varieties: fried, boiled, raw. A lady in a flowered smock is eating at the back of the store. When we enter, me struggling a bit with the door and wheelchair, she comes over to help.

Lilia points to her mouth, indicating that the woman has some food on her face.

"Sorry," I say in Japanese, apologizing for my daughter's rudeness.

She shrugs it off good-naturedly and shows us to a table with a view of an amateur painting of Mt. Fuji. Talk-radio blares from a corner. A few other customers are also having early supper, most of them young women.

"I want to come here some day with my friends," Lilia signs.

At first, I'm startled by her pronouncement. I imagined taking more trips with my daughter. We'd go to Italy! To England! To Denmark! But lately she seems to be more interested in doing things with her friends. Maybe I will lose my traveling companion.

Then again, maybe that's okay. I want for her to be independent. I want her to have a rich life, even without me. Now that she knows this island is here, she can return. She can visit Naoshima and Osaka and lots of other places with her friends. And yes, sometimes with me.

"You can certainly do that." It's entirely possible. Naoshima isn't all that far away, and if I could make it here without any help, if all kinds of people from around the world who don't speak any Japanese at all can make it here, then I'm sure that she and her friends can get here as well.

BY THE TIME we get home, I have a profound sense of accomplishment. After all, I have driven on a Japanese highway alone for the first time in my life. With a little help from my smart phone, I have managed to navigate a city that I'm not familiar with, and get us onto a ferry, out to a rather remote island,

and back again through darkness and fog. I'm proud of myself.

I'm also proud of my son the next morning when the postal carrier comes with a special delivery letter announcing his acceptance to his first-choice high school. He's planning on joining the baseball team, which his father started when the school was brand new. We hug and I start planning his celebratory dinner.

My sister-in-law drops by later to congratulate him, along with her twenty-four-year-old daughter, Maki, who is about to begin nursing school. Her sister Tomomi lives in Kyoto, where she works with kids who have special needs.

"Can I take Lilia and Jio to Kyoto next week to visit Tomomi?" Maki asks.

It's a three-and-a-half hour bus ride. She's proposing an overnight trip without parents.

"*Ikkitai!*" Lilia says. She wants to visit the Temple of the Golden Pavilion and the Manga Museum. And, of course, she wants to spend time with her cousins.

"I don't know..." Yoshi demurs. He's worried about her getting on the bus and how they will communicate. He's worried that Lilia will be a burden.

"She can go," I say. "We made it all the way to Paris. This is just Kyoto. Everything will be fine."

Lilia will be out in the world.

Acknowledgements

FIRST, I would like to thank the Sustainable Arts Foundation. Without their generous support, this book would never have been written. I am also grateful to the judges and sponsors of the Half the World Global Literati Awards for early recognition, and to the editors of the following publications who published some of these chapters or excerpts thereof in slightly different forms, including: Jennifer Niesslein and and Stephanie Wilkinson of *Brain, Child*; Christine Redman-Waldeyer of *Adanna;* Gail Willmott of *Kaleidoscope;* Terri Nii of *Eye-Ai;* Donna Talarico of *Hippocampus*; Eugene Tarshis of *Wingspan*, Martin Alexander of *Asia Literary Review;* Gillian Dooley of *Transnational Literature;* the editors of the Association of Foreign Wives of Japanese Journal; the Beacon Press blog *Beacon Broadsides;* Kerry Holjes of *When Women Waken;* Rebecca Walker, editor of *One Big Happy Family;* Shannon Young, editor of *How Does One Shop for Dragonfruit?: True Stories of Expat Women in Asia*; Janna Graber, editor of *A Pink Suitcase: 22 Tales of Women's Travel;* Darolyn Jones and Liz Whiteacre, editors of *Monday Coffee and Other Stories of Mothering Children with Special Needs;* Kathy Mantas and Lorinda Peterson, editors of *Middle Grounds: Essays on Midlife Mothering*; M. Darren Lingley and Paul Daniels, editors of *Raising Bilingual and Bicultural Children in Japan: Essays from the Inaka;* and Trish O'Hare, who edited and published *A Girls' Guide to the Islands*.

I am also indebted to my classmates and instructors in the M.F.A. program at the University of British Columbia, especially Kevin Chong, and the members of our Creative Nonfiction class, who offered valuable feedback. More gratitude goes to Helene Dunbar for reading an early draft and her enthusiasm about this project, Leza Lowitz for editorial comments and kind words, Jane Bernstein, Claire Fontaine, and the literarymama.com community, including Andrea J. Buchanan and Amy Hudock. Carrie Pestritto also read and commented upon draft after draft, and this book is so much better because of her. Thanks again to Karen Kibler for her careful copyediting.

All the hearts to Nancy Cleary, MacKenzie Cleary, and the rest of team Wyatt-MacKenzie. Thank you so much for the care and attention that you have put into this book, and for saying "yes"!

Thanks also to Claire Tanaka, Wendy Jones Nakanishi, Meredith Stephens, Susan Balogh, Louise Nakanishi-Lind, Meg Sweeney Ishida, Andy Couturier, Liane Wakabayashi, Diane Nagatomo, and Josh Grisdale for your support, participation, and cheerleading.

I appreciate all of the nurses, doctors, teachers, therapists, and drivers who have been involved in my daughter's care and upbringing. From the bottom of my heart, arigatou gozaimasu!

Lots of love to my parents, my mother-in-law, sisters-in-law, brother, nieces and nephew, and other extended family members for years of love and support. And of course, Yukiyoshi, Jio, and Lilia—you complete me. I couldn't have done any of this without you.

Discussion Questions

1. Have you ever lived or traveled in a foreign country? If so, what difficulties did you experience? What were some of the joys? If not, what difficulties and joys would you expect?

2. In what ways is the mother-daughter relationship portrayed in the book typical? In what ways is it unique?

3. How did the relationship between Suzanne and Lilia change over the course of their travels?

4. Suzanne and her daughter are sometimes given freebies. Although she is reluctant to accept charity, she usually accepts. Why do you think they were offered goods and services for free? What would you have done in their situation?

5. Look up some of the artists and artwork mentioned in the book. What is your response to the art?

6. Should art be accessible to everyone? How do you think that art could be made more accessible?

7. What do you think is more important—preserving historical and natural sites, or providing accessibility?

8. If you could travel with one other person, anywhere in the world, where would you go? Who would you go with?

9. After reading this book, which places would you most like to visit? Which would you least like to visit?

10. What surprised you most about this book? Did it change your way of thinking about travel or disability or anything else?

CPSIA information can be obtained
at www.ICGtesting.com
Printed in the USA
FFHW020808220219
50619462-55996FF

9 781948 018449